THE BEST AMERICAN SHORT PLAYS 1990

Copyright © 1991 by Applause Theatre Book Publishers
All Rights Reserved
Published in New York, by Applause Theatre Books
Library of Congress Catalog Card No. 38-8006
ISBN 1-55783-096-7 (cloth), 1-55783-097-5 (paper)
ISSN 0067-6284
Manufactured in the United States of America

Applause Theatre Book Publishers
211 West 71st Street
New York, NY 10023
(212) 595-4735

First Applause Printing, 1991

THE
BEST
AMERICAN
SHORT
PLAYS 1990

edited by
HOWARD STEIN & GLENN YOUNG

Best Short Plays Series

APPLAUSE
THEATRE BOOKS

To Marianne
who is playful

CONTENTS

INTRODUCTION

The short play in modern literature has made a significant impact on the international scene. *Riders to the Sea* in 1902 seemed to firmly establish the form's durability when W.B. Yeats declared at the first reading of Synge's script: "Sophocles! No, Aeschylus!" Yeat's proclamation and others like it began to etch the short play into our dramatic repertoire. James M. Barrie's domestic melodrama, *The Twelve Pound Look* conjured up all the familiar turn-of-the-century elements of the well-made play but in the iconoclastic one-act form. Barrie's short piece was to become a model of structure and theatricality for decades to come. The commercial viability of the form was proven by Noel Coward. Coward charmed Broadway and the West End with his series of one-acts, *Tonight at Eight-Thirty*, which made history as well as Gertrude Lawrence.

A few decades later, the European theatrical revolution of the 50s was led by the short plays of Jean Genet, Eugene Ionesco, and Samuel Beckett. These works — *Deathwatch*, *The Bald Soprano*, *Krapps Last Tape* — marked the beginning of what Martin Esslin has called The Theatre of the Absurd, a movement for which the short play was a seminal construct. These plays dramatized a vision of a world no longer informed by the traditional logic of cause and effect. In the conventional world that stated, "If this happens, then this results," the dramatist naturally wrote with a beginning, a middle and an end . . . in that order. Such a causal construct determined a neat three-act format where even the most tragic, chaotic action was secured with the latent comfort of cause and effect: If this happens, then this follows, and then this results."

But the Absurd world posited chance rather than logic or predictable intelligence as its informing principle. Instead of giving us a logical episodic story, dramatic action now unfurled in a series of disjointed experiences which illustrated in form and content the absurdity of existence. The tight, immediate absorbing, and captivating structure of the short play accurately reflected the purpose and vision of the absurd sensibility. Esslin, quoting the words of Albert Camus, describes the world view from this absurdist perspective: "Out of harmony . . . devoid of purpose . . . cut off from his religious, metaphysical and transcendental roots . . . man is lost; all his actions become senseless, absurd, useless." A play became a forty-five minute inventive, imaginative treatment of the vision of an absurd universe. This radical vision which first took dramatic shape in the short plays of Beckett and others would become the informing vision of modern plays, long and short.

The short play in America has played a major role in the evolution of twentieth-century American theater. In the summer of 1915, George Cram Cook and the Provincetown Players made their historic discovery of Eugene O'Neill with his one-act play, *Bound For Cardiff*. In October of 1917, the Washington Square Players introduced O'Neill to New York with their production of his one-act play, *In The Zone*. Tennessee Williams was published in *Best One Acts of 1944*, then edited by Margaret Mayorga, before he became the celebrated writer of *The Glass Menagerie* and *Streetcar Named Desire*. Years after his first appearance in this series, he returned to his short plays (such as Lady of *Larkspur Lotion* and *Ten Blocks on the Camino Real*) for much of his material, stamina and muscle.

The play from which *Fiddler on the Roof* was fashioned premiered first as a short play in the 1959-60 edition under the title of *Tevya and the First Daughter*. Edward Albee came on the theater scene with the production of his short play, *The Zoo Story*, in 1960, but he had already debuted in *Best Short Plays 1959-1960*, with his play *The Sandbox*. Albee has returned to the short play form many times, and unlike the other playwrights mentioned, he has never really abandoned the form.

Albee has never tried extending one of his short pieces into a longer work, the way Miller extended *View from the Bridge* or the way Williams extended *Ten Blocks on the Camino Real* to *Sixteen Blocks on the Camino Real*. Some recent playwrights have followed the Miller-Williams impulse but to less salubrious results. *Open Admissions*, Shirley Lauro's tightly wrought short play published in *Best Short Plays of 1984*, lost much of its vigor in an attenuated Broadway version. Aaron Sorkin's wonderful one-act, *Hidden in This Picture*, published here for the first time, was extended to a "full evening" in the theatre under the title, *Making Movies*. The potency of the original had become somewhat diluted and diffuse; the result was not a fuller experience, but a strangely bloated one.

The short play is not easily tampered with. The form is complete unto itself, but many of us like tinkering with it, behaving as if the child should be allowed to develop into an adult. The fact is, as Albee insists, that a play must be as long as it has to be. A sonnet does not become a better or fuller poem when a fifteenth line is added. It becomes a different poem in a different form. We have attempted to collect here scripts that fulfill their own sense of mission; no more, no less. If any one of these fragile organisms is to be pumped up or transformed into another larger creature, let that maker beware.

For many theatre people, the short play remains insufficient. It offers merely a condition, a situation, a moment, a circumstance of fixed and limited insight, an event without resonance or sustained mystery. For James Joyce such was his judgment of *Riders to the Sea*. Padraic Colum once told me that Joyce refused to confer on Synge's play any tragic stature because it fell short "of a certain magnitude." When Colum challenged him, claiming that the keening scene in which the mourners fill the stage with their red petticoats was so overwhelmingly painful that it was the equal of any tragic dimension, Joyce dismissed Colum with a shaking of the head and a flipping of the hand. Aristotle's maxim required the kind of length, substance and resonance which could not be fulfilled within the forty minutes which Synge allowed himself.

Such a grudging attitude remains, and perhaps with some justification. But another attitude should be welcomed. Just as one might catch a glimpse of the truth from the corner of one's eye (as Berenice claims in *Member of the Wedding*), so one is apt to catch a significant moment of truth through the narrow aperture of the short play. Such an experience may not have Aristototelian magnitude but it may penetrate nonetheless with the insight of that epiphanic moment — as potent, one might suggest, as any of Joyce's short stories in the *Dubliners*.

INTRODUCTION

Just as Yeat's Irish Airman foresees his death after acting on a lonely impulse of delight, so we gain an awareness and richness as a result of a similar lonely impulse of invention which informs and nurtures a short play. What we miss, of course, is the tapestry of reverberation, the Gloucester plot which compounds and embroiders Lear's own story; the Laertes and Fortinbras' stories which extend the credence and profundity of Hamlet's own tale. These enriching dimensions are not usually available in the short play. But the absence of that intricate echo in the short play does not mute its own piercing laser-like siren.

Our experimental life is made up of an endless variety of confrontations, observations, and encounters. The short play delivers a fulcrum into that experimental life. It vouchsafes us a brief super-charged dramatic encounter which may reverberate beyond its longevity on stage. It has a habit of teasing, of arousing a desire for more, a yearning to continue when it suddenly stops in its tracks and allows the audience to imaginatively extend the action.

My first experience with *Best Short Plays* came in the late '40s when the series was called *The Best One-Act Plays*, under the editorship of Margaret Mayorga. My playwriting teacher at Columbia, Theodore Apstein, was a contributor to the volume almost annually. He, in turn, had been introduced to the series by his teacher at the University of Texas, E.P. Conkle, whose first play in the 1938 series, *Hawk A'-Flyin'*, was in 1939. My first play in the series, *In Darkness*, appeared in the '51-'52 season, my second play, *Sight for Sore Thoughts*, in the '59-'60 edition. Here, in *The Best Short Plays of 1990*, three of my former students (Christopher Durang, Alan Knee, and Wendy Wasserstein) continue that tradition started by E.P. Conkle. The thread of the narrative is the thread of humanity.

Glenn Young and I are proud to continue the masterful stewardship of Ramon Delgado whose insight and dedication propelled the series through the 1980s. May we equal the eloquence of his selections in the decades to come.

HOWARD STEIN
Columbia University
April, 1991

THE
BEST
AMERICAN
SHORT
PLAYS 1990

Ed Bullins

SALAAM, HUEY NEWTON, SALAAM
(taken from the autobiography of Marvin X,
a work in progress)

SALAAM, HUEY NEWTON, SALAAM

Ed Bullins

Mr. Bullins is Producing Playwright of The BMT Theatre of Emeryville, California. He teaches African American Humanities and Theatre (literature, history and critical ideology) at Contra Costa College in San Pablo, California. He recently co-wrote with Idris Ackamoor the musical drama, *I Think It's Gonna Turn Out Fine*, which was done last year at Manhattan's La Mama E.T.C. and in Japan, and is being done in Vienna, Austria this year. Bullins also wrote with Ackamoor the autobiographical play, *American Griot*, which premiered at La Mama last winter.

Mr. Bullins has written many plays, many of them produced throughout the United States and abroad. Among his better-known works is *The Taking of Miss Janie* (*Best American Play/1974-75/*New York Drama Critics), *The Duplex*, *The Electronic Nigger* (Obie, Drama Desk Award) and *A Son, Come Home* (Obie Award). He is the author of collections of his own plays, a novel and a book of short prose — *The Hungered One*, *The Duplex*, *Four Dynamite Plays*, *The Theme is Blackness* (all Morrow), *The Reluctant Rapist* (Harper & Row) and *Five Plays by Ed Bullins* (Bobbs-Merrill). He has edited two anthologies of plays: *New Plays From the Black Theatre* (Bantam) and *The New Lafayette Theatre Presents* (Doubleday/Anchor).

CHARACTERS
Marvin X (a.k.a. Marvin Jackmon)
Young Brother
Huey P. Newton

SETTING: *West Oakland, a street corner beside the now fallen Cypress Expressway.*

[*A* FIGURE *sits upon a garbage can, in shadows from the project homes on the street. The time is now. The* FIGURE *lights a butane lighter and applies it to a crack pipe. As the stage lights rise, he sucks at the pipe and speaks.*]

MARVIN: [*Smokes.*] Yeah . . . I tried to help him . . . but I couldn't . . . I couldn't help Huey because I was sick myself . . . The Bible says when the blind lead the blind, they both fall in the ditch together . . . The last time I saw Huey alive was in front of this same crack house here in West Oakland's infamous Acorn housing project, right next to the Cypress freeway that was devastated during the October 17, 1990 earthquake.

In 1984 I became addicted to crack cocaine . . . Many people, especially members of my family, found my addiction difficult to understand. "You're so strong," they would say. "How could you become a weak, pitiful dope fiend?" But I did . . . My addiction came in my fortieth year, for many people, a time of disillusionment with life, and certainly it was for me . . . I was burnt out . . . Tired of revolution, tired of family life, sex and women, tired of working in the educational system, tired of the black middle class and the grass roots, tired of religious sectarianism, Christian and Muslim alike, tired . . .

Maybe this is what happens when one lives too fast. You not only get burned out, but you run out of ideas . . . What mountain shall I conquer next? . . . And a voice came to me and said: "You shall become Sisyphus. You shall roll a rock up a mountain and it shall fall to earth, and you shall begin again each day for eternity, since you can't figure out anything else to do, you big dummy!"

So I was a sitting duck for an addiction, that is, a new addiction, especially when I became an entrepreneur and had large sums of cash on a daily basis. Yeah, I sold incense and perfume oils and lots of stuff on the street at Market and Powell in San Francisco. I made a lot of quick, easy money ... And money added to my problems because I hated making money. I actually felt guilty about it and had to do something with all that money I had ... So my friends, including my so-called Muslim brothers, introduced me to crack ... I didn't like sniffing cocaine. For one reason, my mind is naturally speedy, so I did not want anything to speed it up more. I wanted to slow down, relax. My thing was weed. I admit, I abused weed because I smoked it from morning 'til night for over twenty years ... My thing was weed, wine and women. I always said I wanted to die from an overdose of weed, wine and women, but along came crack and soon I had no desire for wine, weed or women. With all my knowledge, I had forgotten the simple rules of life: for every blues, there is a happy song — sing a happy song — it takes the same energy as the blues ... Even before my addiction to crack, why couldn't I think of all the good in my life? Why couldn't I sing songs of praise to Allah, my God, for the beautiful parents He had blessed me with, for my beautiful brothers and sisters, for the beautiful, intelligent women I had had, for the most beautiful children any man could imagine? Why? Why? Why? ... Yes, I know now ... because I thought I was self-sufficient.

I had sat and watched my friends smoking crack, but at first it didn't interest me. I did not like the way they behaved ... I'd come into the room and they wouldn't even look up and acknowledge my presence. They were all staring at whoever had the pipe ... But finally, the devil caught me, only because I forgot Allah.

[*He chants.*]
>   I lost my wife behind the pipe
>   I lost my children
>   behind the pipe
>   I lost my money
>   behind the pipe
>   I lost my house
>   behind the pipe
>   I lost my mind
>   behind the pipe
>   I lost my life
>   behind the pipe ...

Yes, crack sent me to the mental hospital four times ... Many times I put crack on my pipe and took that big 747 hit, and I could feel death coming, could feel my body surrounded by the strangest sensation. I would run to the window for air, or run outside for air. But after the moment of death had passed, I returned to my room and continued smoking ... Once I accidentally cut my wrist, cut an artery. I dropped one of my pipes and grabbed at the broken pieces, cutting me critically, but I was unaware. I thought the bleeding would stop, but it didn't. I found my backup pipe and fired up ... A friend tried to get me to go to the hospital, but I thought the blood would stop dripping from my wrist. It didn't. My new pipe became covered with blood. My dope had turned the color of blood. My clothes, the rug, the bed, the curtain, were all covered with blood. But I didn't stop. I kept on smoking ... Finally, my friend got the hotel manager and he came in with a baseball bat and forced me out of the room ... The paramedics came and took me to the hospital ... Ha ha ha ... after the emergency room crew stitched my wound, I got on the bus and returned to my room to finish smoking ... Hell, I still had sixty bucks ... fuck it!

[*Lights change.* MARVIN *pockets his pipe.*]

The last time I saw Huey, I had gone to Acorn projects to buy drugs. My dope friend had told me Huey was there almost every day. "Oh, yeah?" I said, eager to see my friend. And my dope friend said, "Yeah, dude, he's usually over by the basketball courts."

[*Lights change.* YOUNG BROTHER *enters.*]

[*To* YOUNG BROTHER.] Hey, man, I'm finished with this little bit of crack. You come over here to Oakland from Frisco. I know you got some money. Let's go get some more shit.

YOUNG BROTHER: I'm ready for it, Marvin, man.

MARVIN: Hey, maybe we'll run into Huey.

[*They start off.*]

MARVIN: [*Continues/narrating.*] We walked toward the basketball court ... A brother passed us looking like the bum of the week ...

[*A* FIGURE *enters, passing* MARVIN *and* YOUNG BROTHER.]

[MARVIN *continues narrating.*] ... Now I don't recall if I was looking a hell of a lot better ... maybe a little better, since I was in a drug program at Glide Church in San Francisco. Reverend Cecil Williams was doing everything he could to help me regain my sanity ... [*Calls to* FIGURE.] Say, brother ... don't I know you?

[*The* FIGURE *half-turns and looks at* MARVIN *and* YOUNG BROTHER.]

[*Narrates.*] But the bum needed a shave and a haircut. Something told me this bum was my old friend . . . so I called him. Hey, Huey!

[*The* FIGURE *walks toward* MARVIN.]

HUEY NEWTON: Hey, Jackmon . . . what's happening?

[HUEY *and* MARVIN *embrace. Then* MARVIN, *hands upon each of* HUEY'*s shoulders, looks at him closely.*]

MARVIN: [*Proudly.*] Dr. Huey P. Newton.

HUEY: [*Matter-of-fact.*] Yeah, man . . . So what's happening?

MARVIN: Ain't much, just trying to get some D. You want to get loaded?

HUEY: Yeah, Jackmon, why not?

MARVIN: Well, hold on a minute, let me go cop. [*To* YOUNG BROTHER.] Hey, man, let me hold some of that money.

[YOUNG BROTHER *gives* MARVIN *a bill.*]

YOUNG BROTHER: [*To* MARVIN.] Get a small one, man.

MARVIN: [*To* YOUNG BROTHER.] Okay, man. Just stay here with Huey.

[*Lights change. Music rises softly.* HUEY *and* YOUNG BROTHER *pantomime a conversation. Lights change again, as* MARVIN *returns.*]

YOUNG BROTHER: I really respect you, Huey.

MARVIN: Got a spot we can go to, Huey?

HUEY: Yeah, man, let's go to my friend's house on Filbert. He'll be going to work in a minute. He gave me a key to hold, so I'll have someplace to go whenever I need one, so we won't be bothered.

[*They stand half in shadows, half under the street light.*]

MARVIN: So how you been, Huey? People told me you be down here.

YOUNG BROTHER: Yeah, Huey, I really respect you.

HUEY: Look, Dude, I hear ya . . . I been all right, Marvin. [*To* YOUNG BROTHER.] This brother was my teacher, young blood. Many of our comrades came through his black theatre.

MARVIN: Well, you taught me a few things too, Huey. Remember all them books you turned me on to: *Facing Mount Kenya, Black Bourgeoisie, Myth of the Negro Past* . . .

HUEY: [*Laughs.*] Okay, Jackmon. We taught each other . . . how's that?

[MARVIN *and* HUEY *slap five.*]

MARVIN: Yeah, that'll work.

[*They enter a run-down Victorian.*]

HUEY: This is where I'm at for now . . . Yeah, I know what you're thinking. It's a long way from the penthouse I used to live in on Lakeshore Drive.

MARVIN: [*Smiles.*] Well, brother, I wasn't trying to make any judgements, you understand?

[HUEY *pulls out his pipe.* MARVIN *takes a small plastic bag from his pocket, extracts a small pebble-like thing and puts it on* HUEY's *pipe.*]

YOUNG BROTHER: [*To* HUEY.] Yeah, I respect you.

HUEY: [*Irritated.*] Hey, brother, don't tell me that again, please. When you keep saying you respect me, it's obvious that you are disrepecting me. Now, me and Jackmon are talking. He's my old friend. We go all the way back to Oakland City College. 1962 . . . And I wish you wouldn't interrupt our conversation again.

MARVIN: [*To* YOUNG BROTHER.] Yeah, just cool it . . . Here, get you a hit. [*He gives* YOUNG BROTHER *some drugs.*] If you just sit back and chill, you might learn something, young blood.

YOUNG BROTHER: Well, man, I'm not trying to disrespect anybody, but I got a right to say what I want to say. I don't care who he is, man.

MARVIN: [*Narrates.*] I waved my hand to tell my young friend to chill. After all, Huey was one of the craziest black men in the hells of North America, but young blood was determined . . . Maybe he was tweaking.

YOUNG BROTHER: [*To* HUEY.] Man, you want to throw down . . . we can throw down.

MARVIN: [*Narrates.*] Huey was really getting pissed. I think for my sake, he was trying hard to be cool. But I could see him beginning to move nervously in the style of the panther . . . ready to attack.

HUEY: [*To* YOUNG BROTHER.] Look, dude, I'm not talking to you. Don't get in our conversation again. 'Cause we can throw down . . . You buff and everything, but you gonna have to kill me, 'cause I'm going to try to kill you. And if you don't kill me, I'm going to search for you to the ends of the earth to kill you ... Am I telling him right, Jackmon?

MARVIN: [*Narrates.*] This crack thing is something else ... It always involves violence. I once asked everybody I knew who was doing crack about violence ... and everybody knew what I meant. In rehab sessions ... in jail ... I would ask the same questions ... and the answer was the same ... there is always violence with crack smoking. [*To* YOUNG BROTHER.] There it is, man. [*Embarrassed.*] Just let us talk, dude. What the fuck wrong with you? Stop tweakin', nigguh!

YOUNG BROTHER: Yeah, okay, but you think I'm scared of him just because he was the leader of the Black Panther Party?

MARVIN: [*Ignoring* YOUNG BROTHER.] Huey, how long you been fucking with this pipe, man?

HUEY: Aw, Jackmon, I don't know ... two or three years. You know me, I like to do it all: crack, smack, alcohol, weed ... see what I'm saying?

MARVIN: Yeah, you're what they call a poly-abuser.

HUEY: Is that right?

[*They smoke.*]

Go on, take you a big blast, Jackmon.

MARVIN: [*Takes a hit.*] Sho, you right.

HUEY: [*Gesturing.*] This youngster here must think I'm a chump ... I been on death row three times ... now what have you done?

YOUNG BROTHER: [*High.*] I been to jail, man, and that ain't nothin'. My daddy tells me that all the really bad mathafukkers are dead, man ... Say, I done took mathafukkers out the box too, parna.

MARVIN: [*To* YOUNG BROTHER.] Just shut up.

HUEY: What we gonna do about the present situation, Jackmon?

MARVIN: Well, it's a pretty bad situation. The Black army's on crack. And the General's on crack.

HUEY: We can come out of this, man. We came out of slavery ... see what I'm saying?

MARVIN: Yeah, we're going to come out of it ... or die as a race ... as a nation. It's been five years for me, Huey, five years in the prison of my mind. I caused my family great pain and suffering, brother. I'm sure you have too, right?

HUEY: Right.

MARVIN: Caused my woman great pain, my mother and father, my children. For what? Some hot air? . . . You know we made great sacrifices during the revolution, but this ain't about nothing. What we doing now? . . . You look bad, Huey, you look terrible. We got to recover, brother.

HUEY: [*Sucks at pipe.*] In time, Jackmon, in time . . . got another hit?

MARVIN: Sure, here. We both need to be hit upside the head with a baseball bat, so we can come back to reality and get back on the battlefield.

HUEY: We had to experience this, Jackmon.

MARVIN: Yeah, I know we did. And on one level, I'm thankful for the experience because I've learned so much about the human soul and the human mind, what the mind will do under certain circumstances . . . I'm sure you'll agree we've both learned some things no college in the world could teach us.

HUEY: You right. People do some pretty scandalous stuff on this crack. I've done some scandalous stuff myself . . . What about you, young blood?

YOUNG BROTHER: Yeah, I have too.

MARVIN: [*Narrating.*] I used the parable of the man who was crucified, put into a tomb, but mysteriously, the rock was removed and the man came out, came back to life. And not only was he resurrected, but he ascended.

[*To* HUEY *and* YOUNG BROTHER.] He ascended.

HUEY: Teach, Brother Jackmon.

MARVIN: Aw, man . . . I see this crack as the last weapon in the devil's arsenal for the Black nation . . . When we overcome this, he'll never be able to come at us again, not in this world or the next.

HUEY: On a lighter note, have you seen you-know-who lately?

MARVIN: [*Smiles.*] Your buddy?

HUEY: [*Playing.*] Naw, Jackmon, your buddy.

MARVIN: Don't see him much anymore. He tweaks too hard for me, gets real paranoid, thinks the FBI is following him . . . He be down here in Acorn buying dope. You'll run into him.

HUEY: I don't want to run into that cat. Eldridge Cleaver is out to lunch.

MARVIN: Huey, I have to tell you this. I was riding with him one day . . . you know he drives with dope in one hand and his pipe in the other. He said, "Man, you think the police is following us?" . . . Nigguh, hell naw, I said . . . ain't no police following you. For what? They want you to keep smoking. If they following you, they doing it to bring you some more dope. . . Eldridge said, "Man, if somebody else had told me that, I wouldn't have believed it." . . . The boy is sick, Huey, he's illing, and he's skinny as an Ethiopian. I can't deal with him . . . I wouldn't care if he had a house full of cocaine, I wouldn't want one hit from him . . . Think you and him will ever get together?

HUEY: Not in this life, Jackmon.

MARVIN: Why not?

HUEY: [Serious.] It's like this, man . . . [Pauses, takes deep breath.] Too many people lost their lives behind Eldridge. There's too much blood on the path between us, man. Too much blood. So even though I might want to get together with him . . . out of respect to the loved ones of those comrades who went down, I cannot deal with him. I will not deal with him.

MARVIN: Why not, Huey? . . . Hell, Arabs kill each other in Lebanon and Jordan, but the next day they're in the mosque praying together. King Hussein of Jordan massacred Palestinians, but Yassir Arafat is still talking with him. Why can't Black men come together in spite of the past?

HUEY: Not in this life, Jackmon, not in this life . . .

MARVIN: Change the channel, brother. You know our community needs signs and symbols of unity. You see what condition our youths are in. [Points to YOUNG BROTHER.] Look at this fool sitting over there.

HUEY: Yeah, I know they disrespect us, Jackmon.

MARVIN: You're the general, get on your post, soldier. And I got to do the same thing or we're going to suffer a severe chastisement . . . we're suffering one right now.

HUEY: Right. The army is here, but with no discipline, no ideology, no program. We got to get back on the battlefield . . .

MARVIN: Yeah, before the battle is over. [*He stands to leave.*] Well, Huey, we got to get back to the City.

HUEY: You staying in Frisco?

MARVIN: Yeah, for a minute. I'm in a drug program at Glide Church.

HUEY: Reverend Cecil Williams?

MARVIN: Yeah. Trying to get off crack. I blew it today.

HUEY: You know what they say, "one day at a time." But how's Cecil doing?

MARVIN: Man, the brother is trying to deal with us crack heads.

HUEY: He's got a hellava job.

MARVIN: Think he ain't? But he's trying his best, if we don't give him a nervous breakdown. He's a good brother, man, a real good brother. He loves me, man, gives me anything I ask him for, but he don't want to be no co-dependent . . . So we outta here, Huey.

[*They all shake hands.*]

HUEY: [*To* YOUNG BROTHER.] Take it easy, youngster. If you can be on death row three times and come out, you'll be a bad mathafukker like me.

YOUNG BROTHER: Sho, you right.

MARVIN: I'll run into you again, Huey.

HUEY: Yeah, get back with me, Jackmon.

MARVIN: As-Salaam-Alaikum.

HUEY: Wa alaikum-salaam.

[MARVIN *and* YOUNG BROTHER *turn and exit the space. Light off of* HUEY, *looking after them.*]

[*Light on* MARVIN.]

MARVIN: [*Narrates.*] We made our way through Acorn projects, crossing the Cypress freeway that would soon come tumbling down, and entered the West Oakland BART station for the ride back to Frisco, ass out again, with barely enough money to get on the train. While we waited on the platform, I jammed the youth.

[*Light on* YOUNG BROTHER.]

MARVIN: [*To* YOUNG BROTHER.] Man, why you want to upset Huey? Don't you know he one of the craziest nigguhs in the world . . . and one of the most violent?

YOUNG BROTHER: Man, I don't care. I'm a man just like he is. He can end up in a box like anybody else.

MARVIN: You should have just sat there and listened.

YOUNG BROTHER: That nigguh can't stop me from talking. I ain't no chump.

MARVIN: That ain't the point. The point is to learn something from someone who took things to the bus stop and changed the course of history for Black people, white people and the world. He armed African Americans for self-defense against the police, the police who were murdering us in cold blood.

YOUNG BROTHER: Man, that's history. Now he ain't nothing but a dope fiend. So he can't tell me nothing.

MARVIN: Okay, man, change the channel.

[*Lights down on* YOUNG BROTHER. MARVIN *stands in his light and narrates.*]

MARVIN: [*Continuing.*] When we sat on the train, I thought about my friend, Huey P. Newton . . . Little did I know that this would be the last time I would see him alive . . . He was found murdered near the Cypress freeway on August 22, 1989.

For those of us still addicted to crack cocaine, we should feel blessed that we're still alive and have the chance to save our souls, for the sake of ourselves, our families and our community . . . I have no doubt that I will fully recover from crack. Each day I get stronger and stronger. I shall return to the battlefield. I have no choice except to fight or die. For sure, the Black Nation is at war with America. America is using chemical and germ warfare against us — crack, AIDS — along with an infinite supply of guns for our self-destruction.

The main weapon we have is our spirit. We must reclaim our spirit, which is the spirit of God. We are in Him and He is in us. When we forget this, we fall victim to the great lie that all is lost. Yeah, it's raining now, but look, see the sun coming through the clouds. See the rainbow?

Rise, my people. Rise from the projects, rise from the hills, rise and reclaim our souls. A warrior has fallen. But we must continue until victory. But the greatest battle is to win our own souls. And for that reminder, I thank you, Huey. Salaam, Huey, salaam . . .

[*Lights down.*]

Christopher Durang

NAOMI IN THE LIVING ROOM

NAOMI IN THE LIVING ROOM

Christopher Durang

Born in Montclair, New Jersey in 1949. BA, Harvard, 1971; MFA, Yale School of Drama, 1974. Author of *The Nature and the Purpose of the Universe*, *The Idiots Karamazov*, (co-authored by Albert Innaurato), *Titanic*, *The Vietnamization of New Jersey*, *A History of American Film* (begun at O'Neill National Playwrights Conference, regional theatres 1977, Broadway briefly 1978, Tony award nominee), *Das Lusitania Songspiel* (musical cabaret co-authored and performed with Sigourney Weaver off-Broadway 1980, for which Mr. Durang won a Drama Desk Award), *Sister Mary Ignatius Explains It All To You* (Obie Award 1980; off-Broadway run 1981-1983), *The Actor's Nightmare* (on the bill with *Sister Mary . . .*), *Beyond Therapy*, (off-Broadway 1981; Broadway 1982), *Baby with the Bathwater* (Playwrights Horizons 1983), *The Marriage of Bette and Boo* (Public Theatre 1985; Obie Award 1985) and *Laughing Wild* (Playwrights Horizons 1987). All of his plays have had many productions in the United States and abroad.

Mr. Durang has completed four screenplays: for the Ladd Company (co-authored with Wendy Wasserstein), Warner Brothers, the Swann Group (a screenplay of *Sister Mary . . .*), and a new screenplay for Herbert Ross. For television he has written *Carol and Carl and Whoopie and Robin* (for Carol Burnett) and for PBS' *Trying Times*, a teleplay called *The Visit* directed by Alan Arkin. He is presently creating a sitcom for the Fox network. Along with having acted on stage in plays of his own and others, he acted in the films *The Secret of My Success*, *Mr. North*, and the forthcoming *The Butcher's Wife*.

Mr. Durang is a member of the Dramatists Guild Council, a member of the Artistic board of Playwrights Horizons and a member of the Play Selection Committee for the Young Playwrights Festival from 1984 to the present. He has directed readings of new playwrights at the Young Playwrights Festival, Playwrights Horizons and NYU. From 1981 to 1982 he served as King of France. Awards and honors include: CBS Playwriting Fellowship (in residence at Yale Repertory Theatre); Rockefeller Foundation grant (in residence at Arena Stage, Washington, D.C.); Guggenheim grant; Lecomte du Nouy Foundation grant; and the Kenyon Festival Theatre Playwriting Prize.

A collection of his work, *Christopher Durang Explains It All For You*, originally published by Avon, has been re-published by Grove Press. Grove Press has also published *Bette and Boo* and *Laughing Wild*.

He is also one-third of the cabaret act, *Chris Durang and Dawne*.

SCENE: *A living room. Enter* NAOMI, *followed by* JOHN *and* JOHNNA, *an attractive young couple.* JOHN *has a moustache and is dressed in a suit and tie.* JOHNNA *is wearing a dress with a string of pearls.* NAOMI, *though, looks odd.* NAOMI *plants herself somewhere definitive — by the mantlepiece, for instance — and gestures out toward the room.*

NAOMI: And this is the living room. And you've seen the dining room, and the bedroom, and the bathroom.

JOHN: Yes, I know. I used to live here.

NAOMI: The dining room is where we dine. The bedroom is where we go to bed. The bathroom is where we take a bath. The kitchen is where we . . . cook. That doesn't sound right. The kitchen is where we . . . collect kitsch. Hummel figurines, Statue of Liberty salt and pepper shakers, underpants that say Home of the Whopper, and so on. Kitsch. The kitchen is where we look at kitsch. The laundry room is where we do laundry. And the living room is where Hubert and I do all of our living. Our major living. So that's the living room.

JOHNNA: What do you use the cellar for?

NAOMI: [*Suspicious.*] What?

JOHNNA: What do you use the cellar for?

NAOMI: We use the cellar to . . . we go to the cellar to . . . replenish our cells. We go to the attic to . . . practice our tics, our facial tics. [*Her face contorts variously.*] And we go to the carport, to port the car. Whew! Please don't ask me any more questions, I'm afraid I may not have the strength to find the answers. [*Laughs uproariously.*] Please, sit down, don't let my manner make you uncomfortable. Sit on one of the sitting devices, we use them for sitting in the living room.

[*There is a couch and one chair to choose from.* JOHN *and* JOHNNA *go to sit on the couch.*]

NAOMI: [*Screams at them:*] DON'T SIT THERE, I WANT TO SIT THERE!!!

[JOHN *and* JOHNNA *stand and look frightened.* NAOMI *charges over to the couch, and* JOHN *and* JOHNNA *almost have to run to avoid being sat on by her.*]

Shits! Ingrates! It's my house, it's my living room. I didn't ask you, I can ask you to leave.

[JOHN *and* JOHNNA *are still standing, and start to maybe edge out of the room.*]

No, no, sit down. Please, make yourselves at home, this is the living room, it's where Rupert and I do all our living.

[*There's only one chair, so with some hesitation* JOHNNA *sits in the chair, and* JOHN *stands behind her.*]

[NAOMI *stretches her arms out on the couch.*] Wow. Boy oh boy. I need a big couch to sit on because I'M A BIG PERSONALITY!!!! [*Laughs uproariously.*] Tell me, are you two ever going to speak, or do I just have to go on and on by myself, or WHAT!!!!!!

[NAOMI *stares at* JOHN *and* JOHNNA *intensely. They hesitate but then speak.*]

JOHNNA: This is a very comfortable chair. I love it.

JOHN: Yes, thank you.

NAOMI: Go on.

JOHNNA: Ummmm, this morning I washed my hair, and then I dried it. And we had coffee in the kitchen, didn't we, John?

JOHN: Yes, Johnna, we did.

JOHNNA: [*Pause, doesn't know what else to say.*] And I love sitting in this chair.

NAOMI: I think I want to sit in it, get up, get up.

[NAOMI *charges over, and* JOHN *and* JOHNNA *move away from it, standing uncomfortable.* NAOMI *sits and moves around in the chair, lux- uriating in it.*] Hmmmm, yes. Chair, chair. Chair in the living room. Hmmm, yes. [*Looks at* JOHN *and* JOHNNA, *shouts at them:*] Well, go sit down on the fucking couch, you morons!

[JOHN *and* JOHNNA *look startled, and sit on the couch.*]

[*Screams off-stage.*] Leonard! Oh, Leonard! Come on in here in the *living room* and have some conversation with us. You don't want me to soak up everything our son says all by myself, do you? [NAOMI *stands and walks over to* JOHN *and* JOHNNA *on the couch. She smiles at* JOHNNA.] You probably didn't know John was Herbert's and my son, did you?

JOHNNA: Yes, he told me. I've met you before, you know.

NAOMI: Shut up! [*Calls out.*] Hubert! Rupert! Leonard! [*To them.*] I hope he's not dead. I wouldn't know what room to put him in. We don't have a dead room. [*Smiles; screams.*] AAAAAAAAAAAAAA-AAAAHHHHHHHHH! [*Looks at them.*] Goodness, my moods switch quickly. [NAOMI *sees a tiny stuffed pig in a Santa Claus suit perched on the mantlepiece. With momentary interest, she picks it up and looks at it, then puts it down again. Focusing on* JOHN *and* JOHNNA *again; a good hostess.*] Tell me all about yourselves, do you have children? [*Sits, listens attentively.*]

JOHNNA: We had five children but they all died in a car accident. The baby sitter was taking them for a ride, and she was drunk. We were very upset.

NAOMI: Uh huh. Do you like sitting on the couch?

JOHN: Mother, Johnna was telling you something sad.

NAOMI: Was she? I'm sorry, Johnna, tell it to me again.

JOHNNA: We had five children . . .

NAOMI: [*Tries to concentrate, but something impinges on her consciousness.*] Wait a minute, something's bothering me!!!! [*She rushes over to the little stuffed Santa pig, snatches it up and throws it against the wall in a fury.*] This belongs in the kitchen, *not* in the living room. The living room is for living, it is not meant for sincerely designed but ludicrously corny artifacts! Kitsch! [*She sits down again.*] Do you like Hummel figurines?

JOHN: Very much. Now that the children are dead, Johnna and I have begun to collect Hummel figurines, especially little boy shepherds and little girl shepherdesses.

NAOMI: Uh, huh, isn't that interesting? Excuse me if I fall asleep. I'm not tired yet, but I just want to apologize in advance in case your boring talk puts me to sleep. I don't want to offend you. [*Screams.*] AAAAAAAAAAAAAAAAAHHHHHHHHHH! I'm just so bored I could scream. Did you ever hear that expression? AAAAAAAAAAAAAAAAAHHHHHHHHHHHH!

JOHN: Excuse me, I want to change my clothes. I'm tired of my color scheme. Do you have a clothes changing room?

NAOMI: No, I don't have a clothes changing room, you certainly are an idiot. Use the bedroom or the bathroom. Really, children these days have no sense. In my day we killed them.

JOHN: [*To* JOHNNA.] Excuse me, I'll be right back.

JOHNNA: Must you go?

JOHN: Darling, I don't feel comfortable in these colors. They're hurting my eyes.

JOHNNA: Well, bring it back.

JOHN: What?

JOHNNA: [*Sincere, confused.*] I'm sorry, I don't know what I mean.

[JOHN *exits.*]

He's constantly talking about his color scheme. It's my cross to bear, I guess. That and the death of the children.

NAOMI: So who the fuck are you, anyway?

JOHNNA: I'm Johnna. I'm married to your son. All our children recently were killed.

NAOMI: Stop talking about your children, I heard you the first time. God, some people can't get over their own little personal tragedies, what a great big crashing boor. Lots of people have it worse, girlie, so eat shit! [*Calls off-stage.*] Hey, John, where did you get this turd of a wife, at the Salvation Army? I'd bring her back! [*Laughs uproariously.*] Ahahahahahahahaha!

JOHNNA: I think I want to go.

NAOMI: Boy, you can't take criticism, can you? Sit down, let's have a conversation. This is the conversation pit. You can't leave the pit until you converse on at least five subjects with me. Starting now, go: [*Waits expectantly.*]

JOHNNA: I was reading about Dan Quayle's grandmother the other day.

NAOMI: That's one. Go on.

JOHNNA: She said there should be prayer in the schools . . .

NAOMI: That's two. [NAOMI *starts to remove her boots, or high heeled shoes, in order to massage her feet.*]

JOHNNA: And that we should have a strong defense . . .

NAOMI: That's three.

JOHNNA: And that the Supreme Court should repeal the Wade vs. Roe ruling that legalized abortions.

NAOMI: That's four.

JOHNNA: And that even in the case of pregnancy resulting from incest, she felt that the woman should be forced to carry the child through to term.

NAOMI: That's four-A.

JOHNNA: And then she said she hoped the mother would be forced to suffer and slave over a horrible job and take home a tiny teeny paycheck to pay for some hovel somewhere, and live in squalor with the teeny tiny baby, and that then she hoped she'd be sorry she ever had sexual intercourse.

NAOMI: That's still four-A.

JOHNNA: Don't you think she's lacking in Christian charity?

NAOMI: That's five, kind of. Yes, I do. But then so few people are true Christians anymore. I know I'm not. I'm a psychotic. [*She throws her boot in* JOHNNA'S *direction.*] Get up off the couch, I want to sit there. [NAOMI *rushes over,* JOHNNA *has to vacate fast. Then* NAOMI *starts to luxuriate in sitting in the couch, moving sensuously.* NAOMI *luxuriates all over it.*] Oh, couch, couch, big couch in the living room. I have room to spread. Couch, couch, you are my manifest destiny. Mmmmm, yes, yes. [*Calls out.*] Edward, hurry out here, I'm about to have an orgasm, you don't want to miss it. [*Back to herself.*] Mmmmmm, yes, couch, couch pillows, me sitting on the couch in the living room, mmmmm, yes, mmmm. . . . no. [*Calls.*] Forget it! It's not happening. [*To* JOHNNA.] Tell me, can you switch moods like I can? Let me see you. [JOHNNA *stares for a moment.*] No, go ahead, try.

JOHNNA: Very well. [*Happy.*] I'm so happy, I'm so happy. [*Screams.*] AAAAAAAH! Do you have chocolates for me? [*Desperate.*] I'm so sad, I'm so sad. Drop dead! [*Laughs hysterically.*] Ahahahahahahahaha! That's a good one! [*Looks at* NAOMI *for feedback.*]

NAOMI: Very phoney, I didn't believe you for a moment. [*Calls offstage.*] Herbert! Are you there? [*To* JOHNNA.] Tell me, do you think Shubert is dead?

JOHNNA: You mean the composer?

NAOMI: Is he a composer? [*Calls out.*] Lanford, are you a composer? [*Listens.*] He never answers. That's why I sometimes worry he might be dead and, as I said, I don't have a room for a dead person. We might build one on, and that would encourage the economy and prove the Republicans right, but I don't understand politics, do you?

JOHNNA: Politics?

NAOMI: Politics, politics! What, are you deaf? Are you stupid? Are you dead? Are you sitting in chair?

[*Enter* JOHN. *He is dressed just like* JOHNNA — *the same dress, pearls, stockings, shoes. He has shaved off his moustache, and he wears a wig that resembles her hair, and has a bow in it like the one she has in her hair. They look very similar.*]

JOHN: Hello again.

NAOMI: You took off your moustache.

JOHN: I just feel so much better this way.

NAOMI: Uh huh.

JOHNNA: [*Deeply embarrassed.*] John and I are in couples therapy because of this. Dr. Cucharacha says his cross-dressing is an intense kind of co-dependence.

NAOMI: If this Dr. Cucharacha cross-dresses, I wouldn't see him That's what John here is doing. Too many men in women's clothing, nothing gets done!

JOHNNA: [*To* JOHN.] Why do you humiliate me so this way?

JOHN: I want to be just like you. Say something so I can copy you.

JOHNNA: Oh, John. [*Does a feminine gesture and looks away.*]

JOHN: Oh, John. [*Imitates her gesture.*] That doesn't give me much. Say something else.

JOHNNA: Maybe it's in your genes.

JOHN: Maybe it's in your genes.

[JOHNNA, *in her discomfort, keeps touching her hair, her pearls, shaking her head, etc.* JOHN *imitates everything she does, glowing with glee. His imitations drive her crazy, and is undoubtedly part of what has them in couples therapy.*]

NAOMI: This is a disgusting sight. [*Calls.*] Sherbert, our son is prancing out here with his wife, you should really see this. [*To them.*] I find this uncomfortable. This makes me want to vomit.

JOHNNA: Maybe we should go.

JOHN: Maybe we should go.

NAOMI: [*Upset.*] How come you don't dress like me? How come you dress like her?

JOHN: I want to be noticed, but I don't want to be considered insane.

JOHNNA: John, please, just stay quiet and pose if you must, but no more talking.

NAOMI: Insane? Is he referring to someone in this room as insane? [*Calls.*] Sally! Gretchen! Marsha! Felicity! [*To them.*] I'm calling my army in here, and then we'll have some dead bodies.

JOHNNA: Maybe we should go.

JOHN: Maybe we should go. [*Keeps imitating* JOHNNA's *movements.*]

JOHNNA: Will you stop that?

[NAOMI, *very upset and discombobulated, stands on the couch and begins to pace up and down on it.*]

NAOMI: Insane, I'll give you insane! What's the capital of Madagascar? You don't know, do you? Now who's insane? What's the square root of 347? You don't know, do you? Well, get out of here, if you think I'm so crazy. If you want to dress like her and not like me, I don't want you here.

[*Naomi lies down on the couch in a snit to continue her upset.* JOHN *begins to walk back and forth around the room, pretending he's on a fashion runway.* JOHNNA *slumps back in her chair and covers her eyes.*]

I can have Christmas by myself, I can burn the Yule log by myself, I can wait for Santa by myself. I can pot geraniums. I can bob for apples. I can buy a gun in a store and shoot you. By myself! Do you get it? [*Stands and focuses back on them.*] You're dead meat with me, both of you. You're ready for the crock pot. You're a crock of shit. Leave here. I don't need you, and you're dead!

[*Pause.*]

JOHNNA: Well, I guess we should be going.

JOHN: Well, I guess we should be going.

[JOHNNA *and* JOHN, *looking the same and walking the same, leave the house.* NAOMI *chases after them to the door.*]

NAOMI: Fuck you and the horse you came in on!

[JOHN *and* JOHNNA *exit.* NAOMI *comes back into the room and is over-come with grief. She sits back on the couch and lets out enormous, heartfelt sobs. They go on for quite a bit, but when they subside she's like an infant with a new thought, and she seems to be fairly contented.*] Well, that was a nice visit.

[END]

Horton Foote

THE MAN WHO CLIMBED THE PECAN TREES

THE MAN WHO CLIMBED THE PECAN TREES

Horton Foote

Horton Foote has written plays, screenplays, and television plays. His plays include *Only The Heart, The Chase, The Trip To Bountiful, The Traveling Lady, John Turner Davis, The Midnight Caller, Tomorrow, A Young Lady of Property, Night Seasons, Courtship, Valentine's Day, 1918, A Coffin in Egypt, The Road to the Graveyard, Blind Date, The Land of the Astronauts, The Roads to Home, Pilgrims, Lily Dale, The Widow Claire, Cousins, The Death of Papa, The Habitation of Dragons, Dividing the Estate* and *Talking Pictures.*

His screenplays include *To Kill a Mockingbird, Baby the Rain Must Fall, Tomorrow, Tender Mercies, 1918, On Valentine's Day, Courtship* and *Convicts.* He received Academy Awards and Writer's Guild awards for *To Kill a Mockingbird* and *Tender Mercies.*

The Widow Claire was included in *The Best Plays of 1986-1987* and *John Turner Davis* and *Blind Date* in *Best Short Plays of 1953-54* and *1988,* respectively.

CAST:

> Mrs. Campbell
> Brother
> Davis
> Stanley
> Bertie Dee

PLACE: *Harrison, Texas*

TIME: *September 1938*

SCENE: *The living room of the* CAMPBELL *house.* MRS. CAMPBELL, *52, is there with her oldest son,* BROTHER, *35.*

MRS. CAMPBELL: Murray St. John just called and said Davis and Stanley had driven him to Iago and were on their way here.

BROTHER: Why did they take Murray St. John to Iago?

MRS. CAMPBELL: I don't know. I didn't ask him. [*She looks out the window.*] The light's are on at Stanley's house. Bertie Dee is still awake. I would call over and tell her Stanley is with Davis, but I never know what kind of mood I'll find her in.

BROTHER: How long has Stanley been acting so strangely?

MRS. CAMPBELL: Well, he's been drinking heavily for a while. He comes over usually after supper to have a visit with me and the last few months I couldn't help but notice he was very full every time he came over. A number of times he would just go to sleep sitting right on that chair, and then after he would visit or sleep for a while, he would get up and say he had to go down to the office and do some work. I don't sleep too well since Daddy died and I would lie in bed after, listening for his car to come home. I would be nervous, you know, because of his drinking, afraid he'd get in a wreck. Anyway it would be later and later and later when I'd finally hear his car drive into his garage. Sometimes not until four in the morning and finally I called Davis and I said, "Davis, come over here, I have to have a talk with you. Stanley is not getting home until four in the morning." "I know that," he said, "and we have certainly to face something. He is behaving peculiarly." "In what way?" I asked. "He is drinking," he said. "I am aware of that," I said, "although I pretend not to notice even when he goes off to sleep right in front of me."

"Well," he said, "when he gets drunk late at night he goes down to the courthouse square and climbs the pecan trees. Someone saw him doing that one night, and now word has gotten around town," Davis said, "and people stay up all night just to watch him." "Does Bertie Dee know about this?" I asked. "Yes," he said. "And how does she take it?" "She told me," he said, "that she hoped he would fall and break his neck." And he said, "I said,'Bertie Dee, you don't mean that.' 'Yes, I do,' she said." [*She cries.*] I'm so glad Daddy didn't live to see how this marriage has turned out. She's very bitter and hard, you know. She does nothing at all to keep him from drinking. "Please ask him not to drink," I said to her the other day. "I don't care what he does," she said. "Think of your son," I said. "He shouldn't see his daddy drink all the time." "You ask him not to drink," she said, "since it worries you so much." [*He gets up.*] Where are you going?

BROTHER: I'm going back to Houston.

MRS. CAMPBELL: Why? I thought you had come to spend the night.

BROTHER: I did. But I'm too nervous. All these troubles get me wild. I come down here to get away from my own troubles and all I hear are Stanley's troubles. Anyway I shouldn't come here.

MRS. CAMPBELL: Why, it's your home.

BROTHER: I lost seventy-five thousand dollars.

MRS. CAMPBELL: You didn't do it on purpose.

BROTHER: How could I have been such a fool? How could I have let Phil Beaufort deceive me so?

MRS. CAMPBELL: We were all deceived. I was. Davis. Stanley. Sarah...

BROTHER: But I was the original sap. I got you all involved. Why out of all the people in Harrison, Texas, did he pick me out to get involved in his scheme?

MRS. CAMPBELL: Don't look back.

BROTHER: Seventy-five thousand dollars!

MRS. CAMPBELL: I never look back. I have two wonderful daughters. One dead. Three wonderful sons...

BROTHER: I am a failure. A stupid failure!

MRS. CAMPBELL: You were president of the oil company for two years.

BROTHER: A fraudulent oil company.

MRS. CAMPBELL: Shh, I hear a car. Let's talk of happy, pleasant things in front of Stanley. [*A pause.*] I miss Daddy. Those were happy times, when Daddy was alive and we were all living at home. "Who's your favorite?" Mrs. Harper asked me once. "I have none," I said. "Don't hand me that," she said. "You have a favorite. Everybody does." "I don't know about everybody," I said, "but I have five children and I love each one just as much as the others. Daddy and I live for our children," I said. "Our deepest wish is to see them all well and happy." [*She cries.*]

BROTHER: Now, Mama. Please don't cry. You have been so brave.

MRS. CAMPBELL: I know. I don't mean to cry. I know everything is going to turn out all right. Baby Sister and Daddy are in heaven, so they are at peace. Davis is married and has a sweet, hardworking wife, a little sarcastic, but I don't let that upset me and he has two lovely sons. Stanley has this drinking problem. But if we're patient and understanding he'll overcome that, and you will soon land on your feet again. And you may not be president of an oil company, but you will be very successful. I am sure of that. And though your first marriage wasn't a success, your second marriage is a happy one. So let's all count our blessings. Let's don't just look on the gloomy side. Let's . . .

[DAVIS, *26, and* STANLEY, *30, enter.*]

DAVIS: I asked Murray St. John to call you. Did he?

MRS. CAMPBELL: Yes. Why were you and Stanley in Iago with Murray St. John?

DAVIS: He was on the courthouse square when I got there. He needed a ride home.

MRS. CAMPBELL: Stanley, your brother is here. Say hello to your brother.

STANLEY: How is Phil Beaufort?

BROTHER: How would I know? I haven't seen him since the bankruptcy proceedings.

MRS. CAMPBELL: Now let's don't bring up unpleasant things. I want us all to count our blessings. I was doing that with Brother just before you came in.

STANLEY: Guess what Davis and I did.

DAVIS: Not Davis! You did. I had nothing to do with it.

MRS. CAMPBELL: What did you do? If it's something terrible I don't want to hear about it.

STANLEY: I called the Houston operator and I said, "I want the number in Houston of Philip Beaufort," and she found it for me, and I called him up.

MRS. CAMPBELL: When?

STANLEY: Just now. Davis took me by the office and I called him.

BROTHER: Oh, Jesus!

MRS. CAMPBELL: And what did he say?

STANLEY: He said, "What in the hell do you mean waking me up at this time of the night? Are you drunk?" "Drunk enough," I said, "to ask you a few questions. Why did you involve my brother in a fraudulent scheme that took all my mother's reserves? You have known us all your life. Why did you do this to us, Phil Beaufort? You are a monster," I said. "I am drunk enough to tell you that. We are all aware in this family the kind of monster you are. You married a sweet girl, named Marjorie Halliday, from Harrison, took her to Houston, bullied and mistreated her, and when her father tried to interfere you stabbed and killed him and hired a slick lawyer to get you off, saying it was self-defense."

MRS. CAMPBELL: And what did he say?

STANLEY: He hung up on me. I'm going to call him back.

DAVIS: No you're not!

STANLEY: The hell I'm not! I'm going to call him every day. I will never let him forget what he has done. Seventy-five thousand dollars! [STANLEY sings:] "In the gloamin', Oh, my darlin' . . ." [A pause.] Where is Marjorie Halliday?

MRS. CAMPBELL: She's in Houston. Dora Vaughn does social work and she says Marjorie and her children applied for relief. She says she has broken. She has married again. [A pause.]

BROTHER: I have failed you all.

DAVIS: Oh, come on, Brother.

BROTHER: I can never get over my feeling of shame.

STANLEY: [*Singing.*] "In the gloamin', Oh, my darlin' . . . " [*He gets up.*] I am going back downtown. I have to write my editorial.

DAVIS: No, Stanley. You have done all your work for the week. You told me that.

STANLEY: Except for one editorial, I forgot.

DAVIS: Do it tomorrow.

STANLEY: No, tonight. [*He passes out.*]

MRS. CAMPBELL: Was he up in the pecan trees when you got down there?

DAVIS: Yes.

MRS. CAMPBELL: Was he hard to get down?

DAVIS: And it's embarrassing, let me tell you. I feel like a fool standing there and begging him to come down out of the tree.

MRS. CAMPBELL: Oh, I hated to call you and ask you to go down there, but I didn't know who else to turn to. The night watchman called me and said he was drunk on the square and we'd better come for him. "I'll call Davis," I said. "I hate like sin to do it, but I will."

BROTHER: [*To* DAVIS.] Did he call Phil Beaufort?

DAVIS: Yes.

BROTHER: Oh, Jesus!

DAVIS: I'm going home. I have to get up early in the morning.

BROTHER: Don't you think we'd better take him home first?

DAVIS: Bertie Dee won't let him in the house when he's drunk.

MRS. CAMPBELL: Let him sleep on the couch. He'll be all right there. [DAVIS *goes.*] He stays here almost every night now. He just goes to sleep there on the couch. I said to Philip Beaufort once, you know, "How could you have done this to us? My sons trusted you. You've taken everything we have in a worthless scheme." "I did not think it was worthless," he said. "I lost too. I am bankrupt." "You will never prosper," I said. But he has. He has prospered. I understand he has a fine new house, a lovely car and is back in the oil business.

BROTHER: Yes, he is. I am leaving Houston, because everywhere I turn I see signs of his prosperity. It's making me sick. I am moving to Galveston, or Dallas, so I won't be constantly reminded of his prosperity.

[STANLEY *wakes up*.]

STANLEY: Mama, I apologize.

MRS. CAMPBELL: Shh, now. That's all right.

STANLEY: I have not behaved like a gentleman and I apologize. Where is Brother?

MRS. CAMPBELL: Here he is.

STANLEY: Brother, please accept my apology.

BROTHER: You owe me no apology. I owe you one.

STANLEY: Why?

BROTHER: You know.

STANLEY: Forget it.

MRS. CAMPBELL: I am moved to tears by the sweetness of you both. You were always extremely loyal brothers growing up. Daddy used to say, "We should be very thankful our boys are so loyal to each other. They never think of themselves first, but only of each other. You never see one without the other."

STANLEY: [*Singing.*] "In the gloamin', Oh my darlin' . . . " [*A pause.*] I want to start all over. I want you and me and Davis to move back in here and start all over.

MRS. CAMPBELL: What about the girls?

STANLEY: What about them?

MRS. CAMPBELL: Don't you want them here too, with you starting all over?

STANLEY: Baby Sister is dead. Sarah is married to Wesley Cox and you know about Wesley Cox and Bertie Dee.

MRS. CAMPBELL: Oh, my God! Don't start that, Stanley!

STANLEY: I called him up too. I said, "Wesley Cox, I know all about you and Bertie Dee."

MRS. CAMPBELL: Oh, my God!

STANLEY: Let's start all over. Sarah, Baby Sister, Davis, Brother and me. How do you do that?

BROTHER: What?

STANLEY: Start all over.

BROTHER: I don't know.

STANLEY: [*Singing.*] "In the gloamin', Oh my darlin' . . . "

[BERTIE DEE, *30, enters.*]

MRS. CAMPBELL: Hello, Bertie Dee. Stanley just got here. Davis brought him. He was very tired so I told him to spend the night on the couch here. I was going to call you and tell you. I knew you hadn't gone to bed because your light was still on. Davis just left. He has to get up at five-thirty every morning. Brother, Stanley and I were just having a little talk about old times. Brother, say hello to Bertie Dee.

BROTHER: Hello, Bertie Dee. How's Son?

BERTIE DEE: Son is all right.

BROTHER: I guess he's grown quite a bit since I saw him last.

BERTIE DEE: I don't remember when you saw him last.

BROTHER: It's been at least three months. Is he asleep?

BERTIE DEE: Yes.

BROTHER: It seems every time I come to visit Mama, he's asleep.

BERTIE DEE: Stanley . . . [*He doesn't answer.*] Stanley . . .

MRS. CAMPBELL: I think he's asleep, Bertie Dee. He was very tired. Davis said he was working late meeting a deadline for the paper.

BERTIE DEE: Stanley, don't play possum with me. [*She goes over to him. She shakes him.*] Open your eyes! I said don't play possum with me. You don't fool me.

MRS. CAMPBELL: Stanley, are you asleep? See, I think he is asleep.

BERTIE DEE: He is not. He's pretending.

BROTHER: How is your father, Bertie Dee?

BERTIE DEE: What?

BROTHER: How is your father?

BERTIE DEE: He's all right.

MRS. CAMPBELL: Daddy and Mr. Graham were the closest of friends. They had coffee every morning together and every afternoon. They would go to Outlar's Drugstore in the morning for their coffee and to Rugeley's in the afternoon, so as not to hurt anyone's feelings. Their fondest wish was to see Bertie Dee and Stanley married. That was a happy day for the both of them, for all of us, let me tell you. Everyone said, "Aren't they young to be married?" I was married to Daddy at sixteen. We had many happy years together. If you remember, it was Mr. Graham who came here to tell me Daddy had died. He was crying like his heart would break, he was crying so he could hardly speak the words. He grieved so, Mr. Graham said, he lost ten pounds.

BROTHER: Bertie Dee, how is your mother?

BERTIE DEE: What?

BROTHER: How is your mother?

BERTIE DEE: She's all right.

MRS. CAMPBELL: She is a homebody just like me. Neither of us care for society.

BERTIE DEE: I'm not leaving here, Stanley, until you talk to me.

MRS. CAMPBELL: What do you want to talk about, Bertie Dee? Can't it wait until morning?

BERTIE DEE: No!

BROTHER: Maybe we should go into the other room, Mama, so they can have a private conversation.

BERTIE DEE: No. You both stay here. I want you to be witnesses to this conversation. [*She goes to* STANLEY. *She shakes him.*] Stanley! Open your eyes! [*He does so.*]

STANLEY: Well? . . .

BERTIE DEE: Are you crazy? I think he is. I think he should be locked up in the asylum in Austin.

MRS. CAMPBELL: Now don't say that, Bertie Dee.

BERTIE DEE: I do. Do you know what he just did? He called Wesley Cox in Port Arthur, waked him out of a sound sleep to accuse him of having an affair with me.

MRS. CAMPBELL: Oh, my God!

BERTIE DEE: He's crazy! He's insane!

STANLEY: Wesley Cox, Robert Ferguson, Willy Davis, I've called them all. I've called them all and told them no wool was being pulled over my eyes.

BERTIE DEE: He's insane, he's crazy, stark raving mad! Your son, your precious son, is crazy, insane!

MRS. CAMPBELL: He didn't know what he was doing or saying in the condition he's in. I'll get him to call them all up in the morning and explain the condition he was in. I'll call Wesley Cox now myself, to explain. Wesley Cox is very understanding. He's a fine boy, like one of my own sons. Now you go home and get your rest, and Stanley will get his rest, and in the morning I'll have a good long talk with Stanley. And Davis will and Brother will and I am sure we can once and for all get him to see how foolishly he is behaving. [*A pause.*] We all have our troubles. Mrs. Lehigh was here this afternoon to tell me about the Jacksons. She said she thought it would make me feel better to learn that we were not the only ones taken advantage of by a crook. It seems that Mrs. Stone Taylor was having an affair with Mr. Haus and she and Mr. Stone Taylor were closest friends of the Jacksons. Of course, many people thought that Mr. Jackson and Mrs. Stone Taylor had had an affair earlier. Anyway, Mr. Haus and Mrs. Stone Taylor got the Jacksons to invest four hundred thousand dollars of the money Mrs. Jackson had inherited from her father and they made Mr. Jackson vice-president of some corporation Mr. Haus was president of ... and ...

[BERTIE DEE *cries.*]

BERTIE DEE: I'm going crazy. I'm the one that's going crazy. I'm the one that will end up in the Austin insane asylum.

MRS. CAMPBELL: Now, now ... it's going to be all right. Your father was Daddy's first friend here, you know. His first friend and his best friend. When he came here to start the paper he came home that first week and he said, "I've met the nicest fellow, name of Graham. And guess what?" he said. "He has the prettiest little girl, nine years old." And he looked over at Stanley, who was lying on the couch just as he is now, and he said, "I think she's just about right for Stanley." And Stanley blushed so we all had a good laugh.

BERTIE DEE: What's my life like? Married to a man drunk all the time?

MRS. CAMPBELL: Not all the time, honey. I'm very sensitive to his being in that condition and sometimes he comes over here and I smell nothing on his breath. I tell him if only he knew how wise and intelligent he is when sober ...

BERTIE DEE: Getting drunk, climbing pecan trees . . .

STANLEY: I want to start all over again. I want me and Davis and Brother all living here again, so we can start all over . . .

[BERTIE DEE *gets up*.]

BERTIE DEE: I'm going home. [*She leaves.* STANLEY *gets up*.]

STANLEY: I'm going home too.

MRS. CAMPBELL: Are you sure she'll let you in, Stanley?

STANLEY: I'm sure. [*He leaves*.]

[MRS. CAMPBELL *goes to the window*.]

MRS. CAMPBELL: I hope she'll let him in, but I doubt it.

BROTHER: She did have an affair with Wesley Cox.

MRS. CAMPBELL: Change the subject please. I don't care to hear that. I knew it. She won't let him in.

BROTHER: Where will he go?

MRS. CAMPBELL: He'll come back here. [*She walks away from the window*.] I don't want him to think I was spying on him. That would embarrass him if he thought we were watching. When he comes back in here, we'll just pretend like we didn't know what had happened.

BROTHER: What happened to the Jacksons?

MRS. CAMPBELL: The Jacksons? Oh, yes. Well, that Mr. Haus took them and their four hundred thousand dollars, just like Phil Beaufort took our seventy-five thousand dollars. They are very bitter and very upset, Mrs. Lehigh says. "I wish they could take it in the Christian way you have," she said. "How did you take your loss so calmly?" she asked. "Because," I said, "I know that money isn't everything. I have my health. I have four wonderful living children, a beloved husband and a daughter that are dead and lots of wonderful memories." Peek out the window and see if Stanley is still in the yard.

[BROTHER *looks out the window*.]

BROTHER: No.

[STANLEY *comes back in*.]

MRS. CAMPBELL: Hello, Son. Glad you came back. [STANLEY *doesn't answer. He goes to the window and looks out.*] Do you all remember when Daddy built this house? We came here with nothing from Lake Charles and we rented a sweet little frame house across from the Cochrans, and I was certainly very happy there, but one day Daddy came in and he said, "Guess what? I am going to build you a two-story brick house on a nice lot and it will have everything in it you ever wanted, rooms for all the children and a big living room with a piano so they can bring their friends and sing and dance." "Won't it be very expensive, Daddy?" I said. "Yes," he said, "but I want to do it." And he did. And I thought it would take all our money and it did. But when Daddy died, I found that he had seventy-five thousand in insurance money and we were rich . . .

BROTHER: Rich, until Phil Beaufort convinced me to ask you for it to invest in his worthless schemes.

MRS. CAMPBELL: Don't look back now, don't look back. And if you do only think of the pleasant things. . . . When Stanley married Bertie Dee, Daddy said, "I want them living right next door to us. I am going to the bank and arrange a loan so they can build their house." And he did.

STANLEY: [*Singing.*] "In the gloamin', Oh, my darlin' . . ."

MRS. CAMPBELL: "Because we have been so happy in our house I want them to have a house of their own to be happy in," Daddy said.

STANLEY: You know what I just saw?

BROTHER: What?

STANLEY: I just saw my brother-in-law, Wesley Cox, go into my house. What do you think of that?

BROTHER: I don't think anything of it, because you couldn't have seen him. Wesley Cox is ninety miles away in Port Arthur.

STANLEY: Who did I see go in there if it wasn't Wesley Cox?

BROTHER: No one went in there, Stanley.

STANLEY: They go in there all the time. Ask Mama. She'll tell you. Don't they go in there all the time, Mama?

MRS. CAMPBELL: I don't think so, Son.

STANLEY: You may not think so, but I know so. Do you have a gun in this house, Mama?

MRS. CAMPBELL: Now you know I don't keep guns here. I hate guns. I used to say to your daddy, "I want my boys to be real boys. I want them to play football, baseball, go out for track, but I don't want them near guns." We have had such tragedy from guns. That oldest Beck boy went out hunting with the Peebles boy, who was his best friend, and the Peebles boy's gun went off by mistake and shot and killed the Beck boy, and . . .

[BERTIE DEE *comes in*.]

BERTIE DEE: Do you have an aspirin?

MRS. CAMPBELL: Yes, I do. Upstairs in my bathroom. Do you have a headache?

BERTIE DEE: Yes. [*She starts out*.]

MRS. CAMPBELL: I'll get them for you. [*She goes*.]

STANLEY: Who was it I saw go into my house? [BERTIE DEE *doesn't answer. She looks at* BROTHER *and sighs*.] Was it Wesley Cox? Was it Robert Ferguson? Was it Willy Davis? They are all having affairs with her, you know. Everybody in town is switching. Rebecca and Jack Harris, Virginia and Douglas, Laurie Borden and anybody she can grab, Rosanna and Doc, Jenny and Brother Polk. I could have affairs, you know. All I want. Plenty of women want me. I would name them all for you if I wasn't such a gentleman. Who was that went into our house? Who was that went into our house? Who was that went into our house?

BROTHER: Tell him, for God sakes, Bertie Dee, that nobody went into your house.

BERTIE DEE: It don't do any good to tell him anything. I'm talked out. Worn out. Beat! [*She turns on him savagely*.] Look, mister, if you can believe this tired old body can do anything except get to work in the morning and home at night, you'll believe anything.

STANLEY: I see you at the dances. Dancing with all the men. I see how you hold them . . . I see . . .

BERTIE DEE: What dances? We haven't been to a dance in ten years except the Christmas dance. I go nowhere now, because I'm worn out slaving at the paper, because you're so drunk you can't attend to it.

STANLEY: [*Singing*] "In the gloamin', Oh, my darlin' . . . "

[MRS. CAMBELL *comes in with a box of aspirin. She goes to* BERTIE DEE.]

BERTIE DEE: Thank you. Come on home, Stanley. I'm dead for sleep and I can't get to sleep with you peeking through the windows. You woke Son up just now. You almost scared him to death. "What is Daddy doing outside looking in the window?" he asked. "Is he drunk again?" "Yes, unfortunately," I said. Come on with me, Stanley. I'll put you to bed.

STANLEY: I don't want to go to bed.

BROTHER: You have to go to bed, Stanley. You can't sit up all night talking. We all have to be up early in the morning.

STANLEY: Then go on to bed if you want to. I don't need you to stay with me. Fortunately, I have friends that will be happy to see me anytime . . . night or day . . .

BERTIE DEE: Name me one.

STANLEY: What did you say?

BERTIE DEE: I said name me one. You don't have a friend left in this town that doesn't run the other way when they see you coming. And you know it.

STANLEY: Oh, sure.

BERTIE DEE: Sure!

MRS. CAMPBELL: Well, why don't we just change the subject. Do you know what tomorrow is?

STANLEY: Valentine's Day.

BERTIE DEE: [*Shaking her head in disbelief.*] He's really gone. Valentine's Day!

STANLEY: Christmas?

BERTIE DEE: Oh, shut up, Stanley. You're just making a fool of yourself.

MRS. CAMPBELL: It's Daddy's and my wedding anniversary. If he was with us we would have been married forty years. I want us all to go out to the cemetery tomorrow and put flowers on his and Baby Sister's graves, so they will know we haven't forgotten them.

STANLEY: Who was the best man at my wedding? Was it Davis or Brother?

MRS. CAMPBELL: Stanley, how can you forget something like that? Mr. Graham gave Bertie Dee away and Daddy was your best man.

Brother and Davis were ushers. Sarah was a bridesmaid and Baby Sister was the flower girl. Daddy wasn't here for Sarah's wedding and Brother gave her away, because he was the oldest.

STANLEY: Michael Dalton . . .

MRS. CAMPBELL: What about Michael Dalton?

STANLEY: I could walk into his house right now, even if he and his wife and children were sound asleep in bed, and he would welcome me.

BERTIE DEE: The hell he would! Just try it and see!

STANLEY: Les Hines.

BERTIE DEE: Les Hines. He thinks you're crazy. Every time I meet him uptown he says, "Where is Stanley? Up in the pecan trees?"

STANLEY: Vernon May.

BERTIE DEE: He's dead.

STANLEY: Who is?

BERTIE DEE: Vernon May.

STANLEY: When did he die?

BERTIE DEE: Five years ago.

STANLEY: What happened?

BERTIE DEE: I don't know what happened. He just died.

STANLEY: Well, if he were alive I could go see him anytime . . . day or night.

BERTIE DEE: Well, I can't answer for Vernon May because he's dead, but I know what his wife thinks. She told me day before yesterday that if it were her husband getting drunk and climbing pecan trees in the courthouse square she would have him put away.

MRS. CAMPBELL: He's always been crazy about climbing trees. Ever since he was a little boy. Do you all remember that? Whenever his daddy and I couldn't find him, he would be high up in some tree.

BERTIE DEE: Well, a lot of boys like to climb trees, but name me one grown man, besides this fool, that climbs them on the courthouse square at all hours of the night.

BROTHER: Mama, when was the last time you heard from Baby Sister's children?

MRS. CAMPBELL: At Christmas. I wrote and asked them if they could come here for a visit this summer, but her husband hasn't answered my letter. He's very peculiar, you know. He didn't want Baby Sister to have anything to do with her family. I'm surprised he let us bring her back here to be buried beside Daddy. That would have finished me off, let me tell you, if he had refused to let her be brought back here. I've had many a cross, but that would have just finished me off. [*She reaches for a picture off a table.*] Look at Daddy in his Shriner's cap. I remember the day he had that taken. Oh, it was a happy day for him when you both joined the Masons. "My cup runneth over," he said. "My two oldest boys are both Masons." He wanted you both so to become first-degree Masons, but that wasn't to be. Like I told him, "Let's look on the bright side. They are at least Masons and someday you will inspire them to become first-degree Masons. You have inspired them in so many ways to marry young, to go into business, to build nice, comfortable houses for their families . . . "

BERTIE DEE: Stanley, are you coming home?

STANLEY: No.

BERTIE DEE: Then don't ever come home.

MRS. CAMPBELL: Now, Bertie Dee.

BERTIE DEE: I mean it! Don't ever come home, because from now on day or night I won't let you in.

STANLEY: I'll kick the goddamn door down. Whore . . . I know why you won't let me in, so you can whore with every man in town. That's why I have no friends. You've taken them all with your whorish ways. You think you can keep me out? I'll kick the goddamn door in and I'll have a gun with me when I do and I'll shoot you and the bastard I catch you in bed with. I don't care if it's Wesley Cox or Davis or Brother.

BROTHER: Leave me out of this.

MRS. CAMPBELL: Bertie Dee, I wish you and Stanley could go and talk to the preacher.

BERTIE DEE: Let your crazy son go talk to the preacher. I don't need to. [*She gets up.*] But you better keep him over here from now on, because if he tries to get in my house again I'm calling the law and I'm going to have him arrested. [*She goes.*]

BROTHER: Whose name is their house in?

MRS. CAMPBELL: It is in both their names. Daddy and Mr. Graham built it for them as a wedding present. Remember? He laughed and told Mr. Graham, "I'm going to be selfish and put them right next door to me." He had a dream of one day having you all live in houses next to each other, that way he said we could all go through life together. "And when they have children," he said, "we'll build their houses next to our houses." Well, it didn't work out that way. Daddy died and you, Brother, moved into Houston to go into the oil business with Phil Beaufort. Sarah and Wesley Cox preferred Port Arthur.

STANLEY: [*Singing*] "In the gloamin', Oh, my darlin', When the lights are soft and low ... "

MRS. CAMPBELL: I want you to promise me one thing in front of your brother. That you will never climb those pecan trees in the courthouse square again no matter how drunk you get. You can fall and break your neck when you're in that condition. Can't he, Brother?

BROTHER: He sure can. I would hate to try and climb them sober. Much less drunk.

MRS. CAMPBELL: Will you promise me that?

STANLEY: [*Singing*] "In the gloamin', Oh, my darlin', When the lights are soft and low ... "

MRS. CAMPBELL: He was always the climber in the family, you know. He climbed every tree in our yard. He went down to the river and climbed the live oaks and the pin oaks. Whenever I wanted to find Stanley I would always look for him somewhere up in the trees. "What are you doing up there?" I once asked him. "Trying to get to heaven," he said. He was joking, of course. "Don't fall," I said, "and hurt yourself or you might land in the other place." I was joking, of course. That's one thing about us, I'll have to say, we've always had a sense of humor. We've always had time for a good joke. We've never minded a little fun.

STANLEY: [*Singing*] "In the gloamin', Oh, my darlin' ... "

MRS. CAMPBELL: The main thing is that none of us get discouraged. We have our troubles, certainly. Everybody does. But if we try to look on the bright side as much as possible ...

STANLEY: Do you remember when the old courthouse was there and they had long slides out of the upstairs windows to be used in case of fire and when we were boys we used to go into the courthouse yard and slide down those slides by the hour? And then when we got tired of that we played football on the lawn. [*A pause.*] Why do I get so drunk, Mama?

MRS. CAMPBELL: Oh, I don't know that, honey. I wish I did.

STANLEY: I did go see the preacher, but he wasn't home. His wife was there and she asked me what I wanted to see him about and I said, "First, my drinking," and she said, "He'll pray for you about that, but don't get your hopes up as his own brother is a drunkard and he prays for him twice a day and he still drinks same as before." And then I told her about Bertie Dee and she said it didn't surprise her one bit, no one was faithful to their wives and husbands anymore. She says the things that go on at the dances over at the opera house was enough to turn your hair green if you were a Christian woman. She said she knew of ten women all friends of Bertie Dee's all having affairs with married men, and that the wives and the husbands of the men and women involved didn't mind as they were all having affairs themselves. "Well," I said, "some of them are going to mind one of these days and then there is going to be a killing like when Ted Bowen found out about his wife and the Garland boy, and shot him down right in front of the Palace Theater." And Jordan Buchanan would have killed Luke Goddard when he found out he was having an affair with his wife if someone hadn't tipped Luke off and gotten him out of town before Jordan could get to him.

[BROTHER *is asleep. He snores slightly.*]

MRS. CAMPBELL: Look at Brother. He's gone to sleep on us. We'd better all go to bed now.

STANLEY: Has Bertie Dee gone to bed?

MRS. CAMPBELL: Yes, don't you remember? She left a while ago.

STANLEY: Has she turned the light out?

MRS. CAMPBELL: Yes, she has.

STANLEY: We were married at eighteen. We were married in the Baptist Church to please Bertie Dee's father. The church was packed. She was crying like her heart would break. It was really embarrassing. I said to Daddy, "Why is she crying?" "She's scared, probably," he said. "Scared of what?" I said. "You know," he said.

But she wasn't scared of that. We went to Galveston on our honeymoon and she met another couple on their honeymoon and she danced every dance with him . . . holding him real close the way she liked to dance with everybody but me. And I could have danced every dance with his wife, only I didn't feel like dancing and she didn't feel like dancing . . . [*A pause.*] I have been cheated. Married at eighteen and cheated.

MRS. CAMPBELL: I was married at sixteen. Tomorrow is our anniversary.

STANLEY: Daddy was my best man.

MRS. CAMPBELL: Yes, he was.

STANLEY: Help me, Mama . . .

MRS. CAMPBELL: I want to help you, Son. Any way I can. Brother does, Davis does.

STANLEY: Help me Mama. I'm going to fall out of one of those trees one night and kill myself.

MRS. CAMPBELL: I know that. That's what has me half-crazy.

STANLEY: Bertie Dee and Wesley Cox are having an affair.

MRS. CAMPBELL: Oh, I hope not, Son. I surely hope not.

STANLEY: Bertie Dee cried the day Wesley Cox married Sarah, let me tell you. I walked into her bedroom and she was crying and I said, "Why are you crying?" "Because the thought of a wedding makes me sad," she said. "I cried at my own. I had no childhood, no youth, no nothing . . . there should be a law against marriage at eighteen," she said. [*A pause.*] When I was a boy I climbed the water tower once. I could see the whole town from up there. It was a clear day and I could see everything for miles. The river, the courthouse, the gin, the pumping plant, the houses in town, the farms . . . Help me, Mama . . . or someday I'm gonna fall and kill myself. [*He sings.*] "In the gloamin', Oh, my darlin' . . ." [*A pause.*] Am I falling now, Mama?

MRS. CAMPBELL: No, honey. You're right here beside your mama. I'm not going to let you fall.

STANLEY: Where are we, Mama?

MRS. CAMPBELL: In the dining room of our house. The house Daddy built for us all.

STANLEY: Is Bertie Dee here?

MRS. CAMPBELL: No, sweetheart. She's in your house.

STANLEY: Hold me, Mama. Don't let me fall.

[*She holds him.*]

MRS. CAMPBELL: I'm holding you, honey. I'm holding you.

[*He gives a cry of pain and terror.*]

STANLEY: Did I fall, Mama?

MRS. CAMPBELL: No, darling. You're right here. Beside me. Right here . . .

STANLEY: [*Singing*] "In the gloamin', Oh, my darlin' . . . "

[*As the lights fade.*]

Tina Howe

TEETH

TEETH

Tina Howe

Tina Howe is the author of *The Nest*, *Birth* and *After Birth*, *Museum*, *The Art of Dining*, *Painting Churches*, *Coastal Disturbances*, and *Approaching Zanzibar*. These works premiered at the Los Angeles Actors Theatre, the New York Shakespeare Festival, the Kennedy Center and The Second Stage. Her awards include an Obie for Distinquished Playwriting, 1983; an Outer Critics Circle Award, 1983; a Rockefeller grant, 1984; an N.E.A. Fellowship, 1985; and a Guggenheim Fellowship, 1990. In 1987, she received a Tony nomination for Best Play, and in 1988, she was awarded an honorary degree by Bowdoin College. Miss Howe teaches at N.Y.U., Hunter College and the Sewanee Writers' Conference. She also serves on the council of the Dramatists Guild. Her works can be read in *Coastal Disturbances: Four Plays by Tina Howe*, published by the Theatre Communications Group.

CHARACTERS

Dr. Rose, dentist.
Amy, his patient.

SCENE: *A modest one-man dentist's office in midtown Manhattan. An FM radio is tuned to a classical music station. It's March 21st, Bach's birthday, and Glenn Gould is playing the rollicking Presto from his Toccata in C minor. The whine of a high powered dentist's drill slowly asserts itself. In blackout . . .*

DR. ROSE: Still with me . . .?

AMY: [*Garbled because his hands are in her mouth.*] Aargh . . .

DR. ROSE: [*Hums along as the drilling gets louder.*] You've heard his Goldberg re-issue, haven't you?

AMY: Aargh. . . .

DR. ROSE: [*Groans with pleasure.*] . . . Unbelievable!

[*The drilling gets ferocious.*]

AMY: OW . . . OW!

DR. ROSE: Woops, sorry about that. O.K., you can rinse.

[*Lights up on* AMY *lying prone in a dentist's chair with a bib around her neck. She raises up, takes a swig of water, sloshes it around in her mouth and spits it emphatically into the little bowl next to her. She flops back down, wiping her mouth. She's in her forties.* DR. ROSE *is several years older and on the disheveled side.*]

DR. ROSE: Glenn Gould. Glenn Gould is the penultimate Bach keyboard artist of this century, period! Open please. [*He resumes drilling.*] No one else can touch him!

AMY: Aarg. . . .

DR. ROSE: Wanda Landowska, Roselyn Turek, Trevor Pinnock . . . forget it!

AMY: Aarg. . . .

DR. ROSE: [*Drilling with rising intensity.*] Andras Schiff, Igor Kipness, Anthony Newman . . . no contest!

AMY: Aarg. . . .

DR. ROSE: Listen to the man . . . ! The elegance of his phrasing, the clarity of his touch . . . The joy! The joy! [*He roars.*]

AMY: [*Practically jumping out of her seat.*] OOOOOWWWWWWW!

DR. ROSE: Sorry, sorry — afraid I slipped. [*His drilling returns to normal.*] Hear how he hums along in a different key? The man can't contain himself . . . [*He roars again, then calms down for a spate of drilling. He idly starts humming along with Gould.*] You know, you're my third patient . . . no, make that fourth . . . that's pulled out a filling with candy this week. What was the culprit again?

AMY: [*Garbled.*] Bit O'Honey.

DR. ROSE: Almond Roca?

AMY: [*Garbled.*] Bit O'Honey.

DR. ROSE: Ju Jubes?

AMY: [*Less garbled.*] Bit O'Honey, Bit O'Honey!

DR. ROSE: Yup, saltwater taffy will do it every time! O.K., Amy, the worst is over. You can rinse. [*He hangs up the drill.*]

[AMY *rinses and spits with even more fury.*]

DR. ROSE: Hey, hey, don't break my bowl on me! [*Fussing with his tools.*] Now, where did I put that probe? . . . I can't seem to hold on to anything these days . . .

[AMY *flops back down with a sigh.*]

DR. ROSE: [*In a little sing-song.*] Where are you? . . . Where are you? . . . Ahhhhh, here it is! O.K. . . . let's just take one more last look before we fill you up. Open. [*He disappears into her mouth with the probe.*] Amy, Amy, you're still grinding your teeth at night, aren't you?

AMY: [*Anguished.*] Aaaaarrrrrrrrhhh!

DR. ROSE: You've got to wear that rubber guard I gave you!

AMY: [*Completely garbled.*] But I can't breathe when it's on!

AMY: [*Incomprehensible.*] I feel like I'm choking! I've tried to wear it, I really have, I just always wake up gasping for air. See, I can't breathe through my nose. If I could breathe through my nose, it wouldn't be a problem . . .

DR. ROSE: I know they take getting used to, but you're doing irreparable damage to your supporting bone layer, and once that goes . . . [*He whistles her fate.*]

[*A radio announcer has come on in the background during this.*]

RADIO ANNOUNCER: That was Glenn Gould playing Bach's Toccata in C minor, BWV listing 911. And to continue with our birthday tribute to J.S. Bach, we now turn to his Cantata BWV 80, "Ein Feste Burg", as performed by the English Chamber Orchestra under the direction of Raymond Leppard. [*It begins.*]

DR. ROSE: [*Comes out of her mouth.*] Well, let's whip up a temporary filling and get you out of here. [*He rummages through his tray of tools.*]

AMY: Dr. Rose, could I ask you something?

DR. ROSE: Of course, today's March 21st, Bach's birthday! [*Some instruments fall, he quickly recovers them.*] Woops . . .

AMY: I keep having this recurring nightmare.

DR. ROSE: Oh, I love this piece. I used to sing it in college. Mind if I turn it up?

AMY: I just wonder if you've heard it before.

DR. ROSE: [*Turns up the volume, singing along. He returns to his tray and starts sorting out his things which keep dropping. He quickly retrieves them, never stopping his singing.*]

Ein feste Burg ist unser Gott,
Ein gute Wehr und Waffen . . . woops.
Er hilft uns frei aus aller, Not,
Die uns itzt hat . . . woops . . . betroffen.

AMY: I have it at least three times a week now.

DR. ROSE: I came this close to being a music major. *This* close!

AMY: I wake up exhausted with my whole jaw throbbing. Waa . . . waa . . . waa!

DR . ROSE: O.K. let's just open this little bottle of cement here. [*He starts struggling with the lid.*]

AMY: You know, the old . . . TEETH-GRANULATING-ON-YOU-DREAM! [*She stifles a sob.*] You're at a party flashing a perfect smile when suddenly you hear this splintering sound like someone smashing teacups in the next room . . . . . . ping . . . . . . tock . . . . . . crack-kkkkkkkkk . . . tinkle, tinkle . . . "Well, someone's having a good time!," you say to yourself expecting to see some maniac swinging a sledgehammer . . .

[*Having a worse and worse time with the bottle,* DR. ROSE *moves behind her chair so she can't see him.*]

DR. ROSE: Ugh ...... ugh ...... ugh .... ugh .... ugh!

AMY: So you casually look around, and of course there *is* no maniac! ... Then you feel these prickly shards clinging to your lips. ... You try and brush them away, but suddenly your mouth is filled with them. You can't spit them out fast enough! [*She tries.*]

DR. ROSE: GODDAMNIT! [*He goes through a series of silent contortions trying to open it — behind his back, up over this head, down between his legs, etc. etc.*]

AMY: [*Still spitting and wiping.*] People are starting to stare. ... You try to save face. [*To the imagined party goers.*] "Well, what do you know ... I seem to have taken a bite out of my coffee cup! Silly me!" [*She laughs, frantically wiping.*]

DR. ROSE: GODDAMN SON OF A BITCH, WHAT'S GOING ON HERE!

AMY: That's just what *I* want to know!

DR. ROSE: IS THIS SOME KIND OF CONSPIRACY OR WHAT?

AMY: Why me? What did I do?

DR. ROSE: They must weld these tops on.

AMY: Then I catch a glimpse of myself in the mirror ...

DR. ROSE: [*Starting to cackle.*] Think you can outsmart me? [*He starts whacking a heavy tool down on the lid.*]

AMY: You got it! My teeth are spilling out of my mouth in little pieces. I frantically try and moosh them back in, but there's nothing to hold on to. Then they start granulating on me ... fsssssssssssssss ... it's like trying to build a sand castle inside an hour glass!

[DR. ROSE *is having a worse and worse time. He finally just sits on the floor and bangs the bottle down as hard as he can, again and again.*]

AMY: My mouth is a blaze of gums. We are talking pink for *miles* ... ! Magellan staring out over the Pacific Ocean during a sunset in 1520 — [*As Magellan.*] "Pink ... pink ... pink ... pink!"

[DR. ROSE *starts to whimper as he pounds.*]

AMY: What does it *mean*, is what I'd like to know! I mean, teeth are supposed to last forever, right? They hold up through floods, fires, earthquakes and wars ... the one part of us that endures.

DR. ROSE: Open, damnit. Open, damnit. Open, damnit. ...

AMY: So if they granulate on you, where does that leave you? *Nowhere!*

DR. ROSE: [*Curls into the fetal position and focuses on smaller moves in a tiny voice.*] Come on ... come on ... Please? Pretty please? Pretty, lovely, ravishing please?

AMY: You could have been rain or wind for all anybody knows. That's pretty scary.... [*Starting to get weepy.*] One minute you're laughing at a party and the next you've evaporated into thin air.... [*Putting on a voice.*] "Remember Amy? Gee, I wonder whatever happened to her?" [*In another voice.*] "Gosh, it's suddenly gotten awfully chilly in here. Where's that *wind* coming from?" [*Teary again.*] I mean, we're not around for that long as it is, so then to suddenly....I'm sorry, I'm sorry. It's just that I have this um ... longstanding ... Oh God, here we go ... [*Starting to break down.*] Control yourself! Control ... control!

[DR. ROSE *is now rolled up in a ball beyond speech. He clutches the bottle whimpering and emitting strange little sobs.*]

AMY: See, I have this longstanding um ... fear of death? It's something you're born with. I used to sob in my father's arms when I was only ... Oh boy! See, once you start thinking about it, I mean.... *really* thinking about it ... You know, time going on for ever and ever and ever and ever and you're not there ... it can get pretty scary! ... We're not talking missing out on a few measly centuries here, but boom! And back to dinosaurs again? ... [*More and more weepy.*] Eternity ... Camel trains, cities, holy wars, boom! Dinosaurs, camel trains, cities, holy wars, boom!.... Dinosaurs, camel trains, cities, holy wars.... Stop it Amy ... just ... *stop it!*

DR. ROSE: [*Broken.*] I can't open this bottle.

AMY: [*Wiping away her tears.*] Dr. Rose! What are you doing down there?

DR. ROSE: I've tried everything.

AMY: What's wrong?

DR. ROSE: [*Reaching the bottle up to her.*] I can't open it.

AMY: [*Taking it.*] Oh here, let me try.

DR. ROSE: I'm afraid I'm having a breakdown.

AMY: I'm good at this kind of thing.

DR. ROSE: I don't know, for some time now I just haven't ...

AMY: [*Puts the bottle in her mouth, clamps down on it with her back teeth and unscrews the lid with one turn. She hands it back to him.*] Here you go.

DR. ROSE: [*Rises and advances towards her menacingly.*] You should never . . . NEVER DO THAT!

AMY: [*Drawing back.*] What?

DR. ROSE: Open a bottle with your teeth.

AMY: I do it all the time.

DR. ROSE: Teeth are very fragile. They're not meant to be used as tools!

AMY: Sorry, sorry.

DR. ROSE: I just don't believe the way people mistreat them. We're only given one set of permanent teeth in a lifetime. ONE SET, AND THAT'S IT!

AMY: I won't do it again. I promise.

DR. ROSE: Species flourish and disappear, only our teeth remain. Open please. [*He puts cotton wadding in her mouth.*] You must respect them, take care of them. . . . Oh, why even bother talking about it, no one ever listens to me anyway. Wider, please. [*He puts in more cotton and a bubbling saliva drain.*] O.K., let's fill this baby and get you on your way. [*He dabs in bits of compound.*] So, how's work these days?

AMY: Aarg . . .

DR. ROSE: Same old rat race, huh?

AMY: Aarg . . . . .

[*During this, the final chorus, "Das Wort sie sollen lassen stahn" has started to play.*]

AMY: [*Slightly garbled.*] What is that tune? It's so familiar.

DR. ROSE: "A Mighty Fortress is Our God"

AMY: Right, right! I used to sing it in Sunday school 100 years ago.

DR. ROSE: Actually, Bach stole the melody from Martin Luther.

AMY: [*Bursts into song, garbled, the saliva drain bubbling.*] "A mighty fortress is Our God . . . "

AMY:	DR. ROSE: [*Joining her.*]
. . . a bulwark never failing	. . . Und kein' Dank dazu haben
Our helper he amid the flood	Er ist bei uns wohl auf dem Plan

Of mortal ills prevailing. Mit seinem Geist und Gaben.
For still our ancient foe, Nehmen sie uns den Leib,
Doth seek to work us woe . . . Gut, Ehr, Kind und Weib. . . .

[*Their voices swell louder and louder.*]

[*BLACKOUT.*]

David Ives

SURE THING
A Brief Comedy

SURE THING

David Ives

David Ives was born in Chicago and educated at Northwestern University and Yale Drama School. His one-acts have been a staple of the annual comedy festival of the Manhattan Punchline Theatre for several years. He has written for television, for Hollywood, and recently his opera *The Secret Garden*, written with composer Greg Pliska, premiered in Philadelphia.

Bill, in his late twenties
Betty, in her late twenties

SETTING

A café table, with a couple of chairs.

SCENE: BETTY, *reading at the table. An empty chair opposite her.* BILL *enters.*

BILL: Excuse me. Is this chair taken?

BETTY: Excuse me?

BILL: Is this taken?

BETTY: Yes, it is.

BILL: Oh. Sorry.

BETTY: Sure thing.

    [*A bell rings softly.*]

BILL: Excuse me. Is this chair taken?

BETTY: Excuse me?

BILL: Is this taken?

BETTY: No, but I'm expecting somebody in a minute.

BILL: Oh. Thanks anyway.

BETTY: Sure thing.

    [*A bell rings softly.*]

BILL: Excuse me. Is this chair taken?

BETTY: No, but I'm expecting somebody very shortly.

BILL: Would you mind if I sit here till he or she or it comes?

BETTY: [*Glances at her watch.*] They seem to be pretty late . . .

BILL: You never know who you might be turning down.

BETTY: Sorry. Nice try, though.

BILL: Sure thing.

    [*Bell.*]

BILL: Is this seat taken?

BETTY: No, it's not.

BILL: Would you mind if I sit here?

BETTY: Yes, I would.

BILL: Oh.

   [*Bell.*]

BILL: Is this chair taken?

BETTY: No, it's not.

BILL: Would you mind if I sit here?

BETTY: No. Go ahead.

BILL: Thanks. [*He sits. She continues reading.*] Everyplace else seems to
   be taken.

BETTY: Mm-hm.

BILL: Great place.

BETTY: Mm-hm.

BILL: What's the book?

BETTY: I just wanted to read in quiet, if you don't mind.

BILL: No. Sure thing.

   [*Bell.*]

BILL: Everyplace else seems to be taken.

BETTY: Mm-hm.

BILL: Great place for reading.

BETTY: Yes, I like it.

BILL: What's the book?

BETTY: "The Sound and the Fury."

BILL: Oh. Hemingway.

   [*Bell.*]

BILL: What's the book?

BETTY: "The Sound and the Fury."

BILL: Oh. Faulkner.

BETTY: Have you read it.?

BILL: Not . . . actually. I've read *about* it, though. It's supposed to be great.

BETTY: It is great.

BILL: I hear it's great. [*Small pause.*] Waiter?

[*Bell.*]

BILL: What's the book?

BETTY: "The Sound and the Fury."

BILL: Oh. Faulkner.

BETTY: Have you read it.

BILL: I'm a Mets fan, myself.

[*Bell.*]

BETTY: Have you read it?

BILL: Yeah, I read it in college.

BETTY: Where was college?

BILL: I went to Oral Roberts University.

[*Bell.*]

BETTY: Where was college?

BILL: I was lying. I never really went to college. I just like to party.

[*Bell.*]

BETTY: Where was college?

BILL: Harvard.

BETTY: Do you like Faulkner?

BILL: I love Faulkner. I spent a whole winter reading him once.

BETTY: I've just started.

BILL: I was so excited after ten pages that I went out and bought everything else he wrote. One of the greatest reading experiences of my life. I mean, all that incredible psychological understanding. Page after page of gorgeous prose. His profound grasp of the mystery of time and human existence. The smells of the earth . . . What do you think?

BETTY: I think it's pretty boring.

[*Bell.*]

BILL: What's the book?

BETTY: "The Sound and the Fury.

BILL: Oh! Faulkner!

BETTY: Do you like Faulkner?

BILL: I love Faulkner.

BETTY: He's incredible.

BILL: I spent a whole winter reading him once.

BETTY: I was so excited after ten pages that I went out and bought everything else he wrote.

BILL: All that incredible psychological understanding.

BETTY: And the prose is so gorgeous.

BILL: And the way he's grasped the mystery of time —

BETTY: — and human existence. I can't believe I've waited this long to read him.

BILL: You never know. You might not have liked him before.

BETTY: That's true.

BILL: You might not have been ready for him. You have to hit these things at the right moment or it's no good.

BETTY: That's happened to me.

BILL: It's all in the timing. [*Small pause.*] My name's Bill, by the way.

BETTY: I'm Betty.

BILL: Hi..

BETTY: Hi..

[*Small pause.*]

BILL: Yes, I thought reading Faulkner was . . . a great experience.

BETTY: Yes

[*Small pause.*]

BILL: "The Sound and the Fury" . . .

[*Another small pause.*]

BETTY: Well. Onwards and upwards. [*She goes back to her book.*]

BILL: Waiter — ?

[*Bell.*]

BILL: You have to hit these things at the right moment or it's no good.

BETTY: That's happened to me.

BILL: It's all in the timing. My name's Bill, by the way.

BETTY: I'm Betty.

BILL: Hi.

BETTY: Hi.

BILL: Do you come in here a lot?

BETTY: Actually I'm just in town for two days from Pakistan.

BILL: Oh. Pakistan.

[*Bell.*]

BILL: My name's Bill, by the way.

BETTY: I'm Betty.

BILL: Hi..

BETTY: Hi..

BILL: Do you come in here a lot?

BETTY: Every once in a while. Do you?

BILL: Not much anymore. Not as much as I used to. Before my nervous breakdown.

[*Bell.*]

BILL: Do you come in here a lot?

BETTY: Why are you asking?

BILL: Just interested.

BETTY: Are you really interested, or do you just want to pick me up?

BILL: No, I'm really interested.

BETTY: Why would you be interested in whether I come in here a lot?

BILL: Just . . . getting acquainted.

BETTY: Maybe you're only interested for the sake of making small talk long enough to ask me back to your place to listen to some music, or because you've just rented some great tape for your VCR, or because you've got some terrific unknown Django Reinhardt record, only all you'll really want to do is fuck — which you won't do very well — after which you'll go into the bathroom and pee very loudly, then pad into the kitchen and get yourself a beer from the refrigerator without asking me whether I'd like anything, and then you'll proceed to lie back down beside me and confess that you've got a girlfriend named Stephanie who's away at medical school in Belgium for a year, and that you've been involved with her — *off and on* — in what you'll call a very intricate relationship, for about *seven YEARS*. None of which *interests* me, mister!

BILL: Okay.

[*Bell.*]

BILL: Do you come in here a lot?

BETTY: Every other day, I think.

BILL: I come in here quite a lot and I don't remember seeing you.

BETTY: I guess we must be on different schedules.

BILL: Missed connections.

BETTY: Yes. Different time zones.

BILL: Amazing how you can live right next door to somebody in this town and never even know it.

BETTY: I know.

BILL: City life.

BETTY: It's crazy.

BILL: We probably pass each other in the street every day. Right in front of this place, probably.

BETTY: Yep.

BILL: [*Looks around.*] Well, the waiters here sure seem to be in some different time zone. I don't see one anywhere . . . Waiter! [*He looks back.*] So what do you . . . [*He sees that she's gone back to her book.*]

BETTY: I beg pardon?

BILL: Nothing. Sorry.

[*Bell.*]

BETTY: I guess we must be on different schedules.

BILL: Missed connections.

BETTY: Yes. Different time zones.

BILL: Amazing how you can live right next door to somebody in this town and never even know it.

BETTY: I know.

BILL: City life.

BETTY: It's crazy.

BILL: You weren't waiting for somebody when I came in, were you?

BETTY: Actually I was.

BILL: Oh. Boyfriend?

BETTY: Sort of.

BILL: What's a sort-of boyfriend?

BETTY: My husband.

BILL: Ah-ha.

   [*Bell.*]

BILL: You weren't waiting for somebody when I came in, were you?

BETTY: Actually I was.

BILL: Oh. Boyfriend?

BETTY: Sort of.

BILL: What's a sort-of boyfriend?

BETTY: We were meeting here to break up.

BILL: Mm-hm . . .

   [*Bell.*]

BILL: What's a sort-of boyfriend?

BETTY: My lover. Here she comes right now!

   [*Bell.*]

BILL: You weren't waiting for somebody when I came in, were you?

BETTY: No, just reading.

BILL: Sort of a sad occupation for a Friday night, isn't it? Reading here, all by yourself?

BETTY: Do you think so?

BILL: Well sure. I mean, what's a good-looking woman like you doing out alone on a Friday night?

BETTY: Trying to keep away from lines like that.

BILL: No, listen —

[*Bell.*]

BILL: You weren't waiting for somebody when I came in, were you?

BETTY: No, just reading.

BILL: Sort of a sad occupation for a Friday night, isn't it? Reading here all by yourself?

BETTY: I guess it is, in a way.

BILL: What's a good-looking woman like you doing out alone on a Friday night anyway? No offense, but . . .

BETTY: I'm out alone on a Friday night for the first time in a very long time.

BILL: Oh.

BETTY: You see, I just recently ended a relationship.

BILL: Oh.

BETTY: Of rather long standing.

BILL: I'm sorry — Well listen, since reading by yourself *is* such a sad occupation for a Friday night, would you like to go elsewhere?

BETTY: No . . .

BILL: Do something else?

BETTY: No thanks.

BILL: I was headed out to the movies in a while anyway.

BETTY: I don't think so.

BILL: Big chance to let Faulkner catch his breath. All those long sentences get him pretty tired.

BETTY: Thanks anyway.

BILL: Okay.

BETTY: I appreciate the invitation.

BILL: Sure thing.

[*Bell.*]

BILL: You weren't waiting for somebody when I came in, were you?

BETTY: No, just reading.

BILL: Sort of a sad occupation for a Friday night, isn't it? Reading here all by yourself?

BETTY: I guess I was trying to think of it as existentially romantic. You know — capuccino, great literature, rainy night . . .

BILL: That only works in Paris. We *could* hop the late plane to Paris. Get on a Concorde. Find a café . . .

BETTY: I'm a little short on plane fare tonight.

BILL: Darn it, so am I.

BETTY: To tell you the truth, I was headed to the movies after I finished this section. Would you like to come along? Since you can't locate a waiter?

BILL: That's a very nice offer, but — I can't.

BETTY: Uh-huh. Girlfriend?

BILL: Two of them ,actually. One of them's pregnant, and Stephanie —

[*Bell.*]

BETTY: Girlfriend?

BILL: No, I don't have a girlfriend. Not if you mean the castrating bitch I dumped last night.

[*Bell.*]

BETTY: Girlfriend?

BILL: Sort of. Sort of . . .

BETTY: What's a sort-of girlfriend?

BILL: My mother.

[*Bell.*]

BILL: I just ended a relationship, actually.

BETTY: Oh.

BILL: Of rather long standing.

BETTY: I'm sorry to hear it.

BILL: This is my first night out alone in a long time. I feel a little bit at sea, to tell you the truth.

BETTY: So you didn't stop to talk because you're a Moonie, or you have some weird political affiliation — ?

BILL: Nope. Straight-down-the-ticket Republican.

[*Bell.*]
>Straight-down-the-ticket Democrat.

[*Bell.*]
>Can I tell you something about politics?

[*Bell.*]
>I consider my self a citizen of the universe.

[*Bell.*]
>I'm unaffiliated.

BETTY: That's a relief. So am I.

BILL: I vote my beliefs.

BETTY: Labels are not important.

BILL: Labels are not important, exactly. Like me, for example. I mean, what does it matter if I had a two-point —

[*Bell.*]
>— three-point —

[*Bell.*]
>— four-point at college, or if I did come from Pittsburgh —

[*Bell.*]
>— Cleveland —

[*Bell.*]
>— Westchester County?

BETTY: Sure.

BILL: I believe that a man is what he is.

[*Bell.*]
>A person is what he is.

[*Bell.*]
>A person is what they are.

BETTY: I think so, too.

BILL: So what if I admire Trotsky?

[*Bell.*]
> So what if I once had a total body liposuction?

[*Bell.*]
> So what if I don't have a penis?

[*Bell.*]
> So what if I spent a year in the Peace Corps? I was acting on my convictions.

BETTY: Convictions are important.

BILL: You just can't hang a sign on a person.

BETTY: Absolutely. I'll bet you're a Scorpio.

[*Many bells ring.*]

BETTY: Listen, I was headed to the movies after I finished this section. Would you like to come along?

BILL: That sounds like fun. What's playing?

BETTY: A couple of the really early Woody Allen movies.

BILL: Oh.

BETTY: Don't you like Woody Allen?

BILL: Sure. I like Woody Allen.

BETTY: But you're not crazy about Woody Allen.

BILL: Those early ones kind of get on my nerves.

BETTY: Uh-huh.

[*Bell.*]

BILL: [*Simultaneously.*]   BETTY:
> Y'know, I was headed to the . . .   I was thinking about . . .

BILL: I'm sorry.

BETTY: No, go ahead.

BILL: I was just going to say that I was headed to the movies in a little while, and . . .

BETTY: So was I.

BILL: The Woody Allen festival?

BETTY: Just up the street.

BILL: Do you like the early ones?

BETTY: I think anybody who doesn't ought to be run off the planet.

BILL: How many times have you seen "Bananas"?

BETTY: Eight times.

BILL: Twelve. So are you still interested?

BETTY: Do you like Entenmann's crumb cake?

BILL: I went out at two o'clock this morning to buy one. Did you have an Etch-a-Sketch as a child?

BETTY: Yes! Do you like brussel sprouts?

BILL: I think they're gross.

BETTY: They *are* gross!

BILL: Do you still believe in marriage in spite of current sentiments against it?

BETTY: Yes.

BILL: And children?

BETTY: Three of them.

BILL: Two girls and a boy.

BETTY: Harvard, Vassar, and Brown.

BILL: And will you love me?

BETTY: Yes.

BILL: And cherish me forever?

BETTY: Yes.

BILL: Do you still want to go to the movies?

BETTY: Sure thing.

BILL and BETTY [*Together*]: Waiter!

[*BLACKOUT.*]

Allan Knee

CHRISTMAS EVE
ON ORCHARD STREET
A Short Play

CHRISTMAS EVE ON ORCHARD STREET

Allan Knee

Allan Knee's most recent play, *The Man Who Was Peter Pan*, was performed at the American Repertory Theatre in Cambridge last year. Productions of his other plays include *Second Avenue Rag* at the Manhattan Punchline, *Santa Anita '42* at the Chelsea Theatre at BAM, and *The Minister's Black Veil* at Playwrights Horizons. On Broadway he was represented by the musical, *Late Nite Comic*. For television he wrote the four-part adaptation of Nathaniel Hawthorne's *The Scarlet Letter* and the special, *A Gorey Halloween*, based on the characters of Edward Gorey. His short film, *Journey*, won a Cine Eagle at the Washington Film Festival. He is currently working on a musical adaptation of *The Picture of Dorian Gray*. Mr. Knee is a graduate of the Yale Drama School.

SCENE: *The time is 1910. The place is the workroom of a dressmaker's shop in lower Manhattan.* ELIAS *is putting the finishing touches on a dress modeled by* GERT, *an attractive, lively, enthusiastic young woman.* ELIAS *is the master tailor, a mature man, settled in his ways. He is assisted by* SAMMY, *a young man, hopeful and realistic, with a passion for* GERT. *Outside the shop, carolers are singing.*

GERT: I love Christmas.

SAMMY: [*On his knees, adjusting* GERT's *dress.*] You shouldn't say that.

ELIAS: What if God is listening?

GERT: I hope He is.

SAMMY: It's not your holiday, woman.

GERT: All holidays are mine.

ELIAS: Listen to her.

GERT: I was born for holidays.

SAMMY: You were born to bear babies.

GERT: You know nothing about me. Nothing.

SAMMY: I know you've got a body I love to feel. [*He throws his arms around her waist.*]

GERT: [*Smiling.*] That tickles.

[*They continue working.*]

SAMMY: How about you and me stepping out tonight? I'll show you a good time.

GERT: Maybe in the spring.

SAMMY: In the spring? I could be dead by spring.

GERT: I've made other plans.

ELIAS: She goes nowhere. She goes home. She lives in a dream world.

GERT: You men — you've got all the answers. I'll tell you something. I take long walks. I meet people. I study people. [*Looking at herself.*] Yesterday I met a woman. Had sleeves puffed out to here. They almost draped to the ground. She walked — you should've seen her walk. Like this. With her head high. Like she was royalty.

ELIAS: It's money.

GERT: It's more than money. I passed her and said, "Merry Christmas, madam." And she looked at me and smiled. A radiant smile.

SAMMY: And for that she wants to be a shikse.

GERT: [*Goes to the window.*] Look at them. Look at their faces. Look how happy they are. [*She turns back into the room.*] Last Saturday I walked uptown and everyone thought I was a Catholic.

ELIAS: A Catholic?

SAMMY: How could they tell?

GERT: I went into a church. I lit a candle. I thought, they'll throw me out. But so what.

SAMMY: Did they throw you out?

GERT: No! They thought I was one of them.

ELIAS: Turn around, my little Jewish shikse. [*Looking at the dress.*] What do you think, Sammy?

SAMMY: [*Looking at* GERT.] Beautiful.

ELIAS: I mean the dress.

SAMMY: I like the bosom. How do you make a bosom like that? [*He goes to touch the bosom.*]

GERT: [*Turns away, laughs.*] Don't.

SAMMY: It's only business.

ELIAS: [*To* SAMMY.] Go see if the man who's bought this priceless garment is here yet.
[SAMMY *starts out.*]

SAMMY: [*Turns back to* GERT.] Hey! Wanna go skating?

GERT: I don't skate.

SAMMY: I'll teach you. I'm very good.

GERT: Maybe some other time.

SAMMY: All the Catholics go skating.

GERT: Go see if he's here.

   [SAMMY *goes.*]

ELIAS: [*Continuing to work on the dress.*] Shall I tell you something? I'm getting old. How old would you say I was?

GERT: Don't ask me. I really don't know these things.

ELIAS: C'mon, guess.

GERT: I'm bad with ages, Elias.

ELIAS: Guess.

[*She looks at him.*]

GERT: 70.

ELIAS: 70? I look 70?

GERT: You asked me how old I thought you were. I told you.

ELIAS: I'm 53.

GERT: You look older.

ELIAS: It's true. I've begun to creak. [*He bends, making his own creaking sound. He straightens.*] Still, something in me wants to live. Shall I tell you a secret? Sometimes when I see a woman I like, I follow her home.

GERT: You follow women home?

ELIAS: Mind you, I've no evil intentions. I just want to follow her — think about her — and should she be interested — maybe have a drink with her.

GERT: And what would your wife say if she knew?

ELIAS: My wife — she's a good woman, a wonderful woman. An excellent cook. Her noodles are the talk of Cherry Street. But she's got a very somber outlook on life. Living with her is like living with a judge. I walk through the door each night and cry out, "Not guilty!" . . . Another question. If I were Christian, would you go for me?

GERT: Absolutely.

ELIAS: I don't believe you. An older man?

GERT: You're a man of experience. You could teach me things.

ELIAS: I could . . . Once I followed you.

GERT: [*Surprised.*] You followed *me*?

ELIAS: [*Smiles with embarrassment.*] I didn't know it was you. All I saw was a beautiful woman. It's true, I don't see too well from a distance. So I followed. I imagined so many wild things with you,

Gert. You wouldn't believe. From a distance, you truly inspired me. But when I saw it was you, my God, I got sick to my stomach.

GERT: I affect men that way.

ELIAS: Come here. Let me fix that collar. [*She goes to him.*] You got a very nice neck, you know. First thing I noticed about you was your neck. You can tell a lot about a woman by her neck.

GERT: I've got a secret too, Elias.

ELIAS: My God, it's a night of confessions.

GERT: The man coming for the dress —

ELIAS: The great Hartman. The great liberal.

GERT: I *know* him.

ELIAS: We all know him. He comes into the shop.

GERT: No, I really know him. We've talked at length.

ELIAS: You and Hartman?

GERT: You won't believe this. You won't breathe a word to anyone — not even Sammy?

ELIAS: May my wife suffer shingles if I do.

GERT: We're going away together.

ELIAS: You and Hartman?

GERT: Shh! [*She dances about.*] I can't tell you how happy I am. My things are all packed. Look. [*She shows him her valise.*]

ELIAS: You don't own very much.

GERT: I'm not taking very much. My Jewish possessions I'm leaving behind. I didn't even take my lace.

ELIAS: He asked you to go with him?

GERT: [*Very deliberate.*] He said — he would see me tonight. He said — he had something very important to tell me. Something that would make us both very happy. [*She looks out.*] You dream of moments like this. You think they'll never come. And then one day — [*She turns to* ELIAS.] I heard him speak once. He's a great speaker. [*She recites.*] "Think what is true for you is true for all men and women. That is the stuff of genius."

ELIAS: He said that?

GERT: They call him a prophet. He has a truly magnificent face. [*Dreamily.*] Tonight we'll sing Christmas carols together. And we'll go to the midnight mass. I've never actually been to a mass. [*She turns to* ELIAS.] You think it's wrong of me?

ELIAS: I don't know.

GERT: Surely God understands. [*She turns away. Dreamily.*] When he touches me —

ELIAS: He's touched you?

GERT: Politely. Like a gentleman would. Here. And here. And here. He said — I had the stuff in me to arouse a man's heart.

ELIAS: I think maybe he had another organ in mind.

GERT: [*Turns to him, excited.*] He gave me a book to read. Look. [*She shows him a book.*]

ELIAS: [*Reads.*] "The Emancipated Woman."

GERT: I think he's buying this dress for me. Why else would he ask for me to model it? [*She sings.*] "Silent night. Holy night —"

   [SAMMY *comes rushing back in with a box of ribbons, which he drops before her.*]

SAMMY: Here.

GERT: What's this?

SAMMY: I stole them for you.

GERT: Ribbons? What for?

SAMMY: I thought you might like them.

ELIAS: Put them back, Sammy.

GERT: I don't want his ribbons.

SAMMY: He's got millions of ribbons.

ELIAS: What are you doing?

SAMMY: [*Stuffing the ribbons in his mouth.*] I'm eating them. I'm going crazy. [*He rushes to the window.*] Those singers. I wish they'd stop. They're beginning to get on my nerves.

ELIAS: Did he come for the dress yet?

SAMMY: No.

ELIAS: Put the sash around her.

SAMMY: [*Going for the sash.*] The boss says we have to work late tonight. Can you believe it? [*He puts the sash around* GERT.]

ELIAS: Squeeze her in, Sammy.

SAMMY: Breathe in.

ELIAS: Tighter.

SAMMY: Hold your breath.

ELIAS: More.

GERT: I can't breathe.

ELIAS: Good. [*The sash is complete.*] There. Go to the mirror. [*She does.*]

SAMMY: I propose a toast. [*He fills three thimbles with schnaps.*] To a masterpiece. And a master. Le'cheiim!

EVERYONE: Le'cheiim!

ELIAS: [*To* GERT.] Let me see how it looks when you move.

[*She walks about.*]

GERT: Once my father tried to force me to marry against my will. And when he wouldn't listen to my protests, I plunged my foot into a kettle of boiling water and held it there until it was nearly boiled raw.

SAMMY: [*Following after her fixing the dress.*] Smart girl.

GERT: I didn't have to marry.

ELIAS: Hold your head a bit higher.

GERT: Of course my foot was scalded terribly, and I had to remain in bed for weeks.

ELIAS: Come this way.

GERT: But it was worth it.

SAMMY: [*Taking hold of her around the waist.*] What other outrageous things have you done?

GERT: You don't take me seriously.

SAMMY: I do.

GERT: I still have the scars if you care to see them.

SAMMY: I'd love to see them.

GERT: You could never be what I want.

SAMMY: I'll change.

GERT: You'll always be a small little man working at Hein and Fox.

SAMMY: You're wrong. I'm thinking of going into junk.

GERT: Into junk?

SAMMY: They say there's a fortune to be made there. I've already talked to people. They all tell me one thing. Junk. [*He kisses her.*]

[*She smacks him hard across the face.*]

SAMMY: Merry Christmas.

ELIAS: He's here! I see him walking around.

GERT: Oh, my God!

ELIAS: Get out there!

GERT: I can't move.

ELIAS: Get out there!

GERT: I'm shaking.

ELIAS: Don't shake. Go.

[*She starts off.*]
   Stand straight. Head high, Gert.

[*She goes.*]
   She sleeps with him.

SAMMY: With who?

ELIAS: With that gentleman. Of course, it's just in her dreams. But I thought you'd like to know.

SAMMY: It's maddness, isn't it? It's like the whole world was inside out. Nothing makes sense. [*Returns to work.*] There's a man in Yonkers says he'll give a thousand dollars for the conversion of a Jew to Christianity.

ELIAS: I'll take it.

SAMMY: Scratch a little Jew deep enough and you'll find a little Christian in him.

ELIAS: Scratch a little Jew deep enough and you'll kill him.

SAMMY: I'll make a fortune in junk.

ELIAS: [*Working.*] My wife insists I work. "All right," I say," You want me to work, I'll work. But don't expect love." She looked at me like I was out of my mind. "Love?" she said. "When have I ever expected love?" I couldn't believe I married such a woman. I used to spend my days reading the Talmud. Such days. My wife had a nice little business. Sold manure.

SAMMY: What sort of business is that for a woman?

ELIAS: A good business, believe me. We ate good. We slept good. And she rejoiced in the fact she was married to a man of learning. Now it's all greed. We've got twelve of everything. Twelve plates. Twelve cups. Twelve chairs. Twelve towels. And there's just two of us. I keep asking her, "Who are you expecting?"

SAMMY: I'll never marry.

ELIAS: You never know. Everyone makes mistakes.

SAMMY: I know. I'll never marry.

[GERT *walks back in. The men turn to her. The carolers continue singing.* ELIAS *looks at her. She seems to be in a daze.*]

ELIAS: Well?

SAMMY: Say something.

[*She continues to walk as if in a trance.*]

ELIAS: Gert, tell us.

SAMMY: What was said?

GERT: He wasn't alone.

ELIAS: Who was with him?

GERT: He introduced me to — to —

SAMMY: To who?

GERT: His fiancee.

ELIAS: What about the dress?

GERT: The dress?

ELIAS: What did he say?

GERT: He didn't remember my name. I had to tell him.

ELIAS: But what about the dress?

GERT: He said — he said — it was perfection.

ELIAS: He liked the dress!

GERT: [*Explodes.*] I hate it here! I hate being a Jew! I hate being stuck in this shop! Working twelve hours a day! I hate the two of you!

[*Silence. They listen to the singing.*]

SAMMY: I wish they'd shut up!

GERT: I want to be out there with them.

SAMMY: [*Stopping her.*] I understand your feelings. I do.

ELIAS: It's begun to snow. Look.

[*They look out. The singing continues.*]

SAMMY: What do you say — we go out? The three of us?

ELIAS: The three of us?

SAMMY: Why not? We'll be like Christians tonight. We'll do big things. We'll pretend we're rich, uptown people. We'll celebrate and give gifts. And we'll love one another. Like a brotherhood. I mean for one night, why not? [*The singing continues.*] Gert? What do you say? [*The singing continues. They listen.*]

GERT: Yes! Yes! You're right. We'll sing. We'll do something wonderful for ourselves. We needn't be stuck here forever. America is a big place.

SAMMY: Of course it's big. It's enormous. We'll sing carols.

ELIAS: I've never sung a Christmas carol.

SAMMY: We'll sing! And for one night, we'll love each other. Le'cheiim!

EVERYONE: Le'cheiim!

[*The carolers continue singing, as the lights lower.*]

Romulus Linney

AKHMATOVA
A Play in One Act

AKHMATOVA

Romulus Linney

Romulus Linney is the author of three novels and twenty-eight plays, which have been seen, over the past twenty years, in resident theatres across the United States, as well as in New York, Los Angeles, London and Vienna. They include *The Sorrows of Frederick, Holy Ghosts, Childe Byron, April Snow* and *Three Poets.* Five of his one act plays have appeared in *Best Short Plays, Time* magazine picked *Laughing Stock* as one of the ten best plays of 1984, his adaptation and direction of his 1962 novel *Heathen Valley* won the National Critics Award and appears in *Best Plays of the Year 1987-88,* and his play 2 won the same award for the season of 1989-90 in its Humana Festival production at the Actors Theatre of Louisville, and appears in *Best Plays of the Year 1989-90.* He has received two fellowships from NEA, as well as Guggenheim, Rockefeller, and National Foundation for the Arts grants, an Obie Award, three Hollywood Drama-Logue Awards, the Mishima Prize for Fiction, and in 1984, the Award in Literature from the American Academy and Institute of Arts and Letters. He has directed his plays for the Milwaukee Repertory, the Alley Theatre, the Philadelphia Festival for New Plays, the Whole Theatre Company, the San Francisco Bay Area Festival, the Actors Studio, and the Theatre for the New City. He is a member of the Ensemble Studio Theatre, the Executive Board of American PEN and a Director of the Corporation of Yaddo. A graduate of Oberlin College and the Yale School of Drama, he teaches playwriting, screenwriting and fiction at Columbia and the University of Pennsylvania. He lives in New York City.

CHARACTERS:
Pecdov
Marya
Rudinsky
Klarina
Anna Akhmatova

PLACE: *Moscow*

TIME: *10 a.m. March 6, 1953*

SCENE: *A red flag on the black wall. An elegant carpet. A sturdy table with two chairs on each side. On the table is a cigarette box and ashtray, matches. Two other chairs downstage on each side.*

Morning light. A deep bell tolls.

PECDOV *stands in the light, at ease, relentlessly cheerful.* MARYA *sits. She is terrified, trying not to show it.*

PECDOV: Stalin, dead. Difficult to believe. Hard to grasp. [*He mimes closing a window. The bell is shut out. He turns to* MARYA.] It is about ten pages long. Divided into many sections. A poem. We don't know the title.

MARYA: I see.

PECDOV: It is about a woman standing in front of a prison.

MARYA: I see.

PECDOV: She is waiting.

MARYA: I see.

PECDOV: [*Smiling.*] Please say something beside "I see." It sounds pedantic.

MARYA: I'm sorry.

PECDOV: Such poems, given out in pieces for different people to memorize, exist like that. Unwritten. To be assembled. The existence of this one is alarming. Why? We'll see. [*Pause. He stares at her a moment, smiling.*] Well, old woman, standing in line. Thinking, probably, poetic thoughts. Anything wrong with that?

MARYA: If her thoughts are a danger to the state, yes.

PECDOV: How could they be? Some old bag of bones? But then, another woman becomes involved. She is also standing in the prison line. What does she say?

MARYA: How should I know?

PECDOV: Guess.

MARYA: How the old women could threaten the state?

PECDOV: That's better.

MARYA: They know something. State secrets?

PECDOV: They have no knowledge of anything about the government. Try again.

MARYA: One old woman is the poet?

PECDOV: Brilliant.

MARYA: And the other is like the reader. Audience. You and me.

PECDOV: You are capable of marvels.

MARYA: They have made someone in the government angry.

PECDOV: Exasperated, better word. Would you like a cigarette?

MARYA: No, thank you.

PECDOV: Do you mind if I smoke?

MARYA: Please do.

PECDOV: Well, maybe I won't. [*He doesn't smoke.*] Try again. Personal life. Husband, say.

MARYA: The poet is married to the wrong person.

PECDOV: She was once but he died. You're getting close.

MARYA: She is accusing someone of something.

PECDOV: Stay where you were. Not marriage, but what comes next?

MARYA: Children?

PECDOV: Children. Exactly. This old woman, well, maybe not so old as I've made out, late forties, let's say, and in an oriental sort of way, quite handsome — she has a child. In the prison.

MARYA: Oh. [*Pause.*] Akhmatova.

PECDOV: Good for you. [*Smiling.*] Ever met her?

MARYA: You know I have.

PECDOV: I'm glad we're being straightforward with each other. One of the women in line: Anna Andreyevna Akhmatova. The other an old hag. Then, ten pages of poetry, saying we know not what, and at the very end, something overwhelming. Stupendous. But's all we know. Ever meet Gumilev, her son?

MARYA: After he was in prison.

PECDOV: The first time? That was in the thirties.

MARYA: When I was a child.

PECDOV: Set free to fight in the Army. War over, his grateful nation puts him in prison again. In and out and in, like that. I wonder why?

MARYA: His mother.

PECDOV: Um, and out of her son's tragedy she makes yet another poem, possibly treason. Poets are persistent, I'll say that for them. Now what? [*Pause.*] Do you like this room? It has always been used for these polite discussions. One of my predecessors, years ago, had Turgenev here. He was a young man then. So handsome, enormous shocks of hair. So rich. Mama's enormous hunks of the motherland. A thousand slaves. He had written a story. Do you know what he was told? Right here?

MARYA: No.

PECDOV: Given a brandy first. A Minister of Culture, no doubt quite like me, congratulated him. "Welcome, Ivan Sergeevich, to Russian letters!" "Thank you." There was a moment: Turgenev waiting to hear what was to be cut from his story, and the Minister like me waiting to strike to the heart of the matter. Which he did.

MARYA: I see.

PECDOV: [*Quickly.*] You *see*?

MARYA: I beg your pardon! I don't see! What happened then?

PECDOV: Turgenev finally blurted out, "Well, come now! What do you want cut?" Would you call that rude?

MARYA: Uh, yes.

PECDOV: I wouldn't. He asked an honest question. He got an honest answer. "We don't want to change a word of what you have written." said the man like me. "We just want to break its spirit." [*Pause.*] *You see?* [*Pause.*] Do you have any idea of what I'm saying?

MARYA: Not quite, no.

PECDOV: Well. We sit here in this same room, almost a century later, and I am saying the same thing, this time about a woman who stood in a line in front of a prison and then didn't write down a poem about it. Whatever that is, I want to break its spirit, but I don't know what that spirit is, or what it says. I only know who possesses it.

MARYA: Akhmatova.

PECDOV: But why should I call you in, someone who knows her only slightly?

MARYA: You know I know her very well.

PECDOV: Yes, I do know that. But still, why? To ask you what she wrote?

MARYA: To ask if it threatens you.

PECDOV: Absolutely, and not just in the spirit. A real threat, in revolutionary terms. You love your country, don't you?

MARYA: Yes.

PECDOV: You wouldn't do anything to hurt her, would you?

MARYA: Never.

PECDOV: Do you think Akhmatova would?

MARYA: No, I don't.

PECDOV: How do you know?

MARYA: Her patriotic poems mean what they say. She wrote poems in praise of Stalin, too.

PECDOV: I know she wrote them and I know why and it wasn't for the love of Comrade Stalin. It was to keep her son from being executed. At the end of this poem, there is something else. What? Don't know. But whatever it is, people weep at the thought of it. So moved, they give Akhmatova money. Food. They help her live. What is it?

MARYA: I don't know.

[*Pause.*]

PECDOV: In her early poems there are always lovers. Lovers, lovers. Zhdanov called her half nun, half whore. Do you know many writers like that?

MARYA: I know many writers who would like to be like that.

PECDOV: Artistic wit is so delicious. When a country needs patriots. [*Pause.*] Anna Akhmatova is a relic of the Russian past. Living on, because of a talent, gift, yes, remarkable, for writing artistic ditties. Impressive as verse, perhaps: accurate, specific, surprising, melodious in her blunt way, sticking in the mind. But what is it about? Personal superiority, that's what it's about!! Nostalgia for a childhood in the city of the Tsars, and how beautiful were the pine trees! Young lieutenants committing suicide! Great artists, mysterious doubles! All this bunk steaming in the rotten fumes of sick Christian mysticism, and the stink of Great Art. What could be worse for a Working People than a self-absorbed Nun/Whore Artiste! Our Soviet children, studying *her* in school? Today? Unthinkable! Stalin would get right out of his coffin! [*Smile.*] But I am always ready to learn. [*Pause.*] Who is the other old woman in her poem?

MARYA: I don't know.

PECDOV: I have asked you two questions. What revelation is at the end of the poem and who is the old woman at the beginning. You say you don't know. Can you anticipate the next question?

MARYA: No.

PECDOV: Simple. Have you read the poem? But, wait, I haven't asked you yet. I don't want to, because then if you say you haven't, we face real difficulties. I haven't asked you anything yet. Nothing can be done to you yet. All right?

MARYA: Yes.

PECDOV: You're shaking. You've said nothing wrong. You are a valued worker, a teacher, respected by your students. However, once I ask you that question, then — we're in the soup. Your job, husband, children and so on. Do I have to ask?

[*Long pause.*]

MARYA: She gave me five words to remember. And I know the title. Requiem.

PECDOV: Requiem? [*Laughs.*] Not for Stalin, that's for certain. For her son? Maybe. For our government? Maybe. Only five words?

MARYA: That's all.

PECDOV: Do you expect me to believe that?

MARYA: It's the truth!

PECDOV: Why only five words?

MARYA: I don't know. Maybe she didn't trust me.

PECDOV: What are the five words.

MARYA: River. Cows. Doves. Rain. Statue.

PECDOV: What?

MARYA: Key words, maybe. I think for the ending of the poem, but she didn't say that.

PECDOV: This is all you have to tell me?

MARYA: It's all I know.

PECDOV: Statue. Whose?

MARYA: I don't know that, either.

PECDOV: Statue, statue. There is no statue in front of that prison.

MARYA: I didn't think so.

PECDOV: What else? What *else*?

MARYA: Anna Andreyevna told me nothing else. I swear it.

PECDOV: [*Smiling.*] I see. Wait outside, with the others.

MARYA: You're smiling.

PECDOV: I begin my day with joy, and end it with joy. In between, I smile a lot. Wait outside.

[*Exit* MARYA, *as fast as she can.*]

PECDOV: Hm.

[*Blackout. Lights up on* PECDOV *with* RUDINSKY, *a man in shabby, worn clothes.*]

PECDOV: You'll have to do better than that!

RUDINSKY: He just won't talk about his mother.

PECDOV: But does he know about it?

RUDINSKY: You mean her poem?

PECDOV: No, *the end of the world.* Sit down!

RUDINSKY: You mean her poem?

PECDOV: [*Sighs.*] God damn it.

RUDINSKY: Forgive me, but I have been given very peculiar instructions! Go to prison! Get to know a man! Find out about his mother! I am performing this duty to the very best of my ability but I can't threaten him! I can't work him over! I can't get *at* him! God damn it yourself! I beg your pardon.

PECDOV: Frustrated, are you? Have to know why you are doing what you are doing? [*Pause.*] All right. Stalin died Sunday, after an all night dinner with Beria, Bulganin, Khruschev, and Malenkov. A purge was on. At the top. At the *very* top. Put it together. Well? *Well?*

RUDINSKY: [*Aghast.*] They murdered Stalin?

PECDOV: It's possible. Cerebral hemorrhages can be brought about. Now, a rising Minister of Culture, in my position, does what?

RUDINSKY: Something threatening none of them.

PECDOV: Of course, but what?

RUDINSKY: Nothing?

PECDOV: Fatal. It would be like I was waiting.

RUDINSKY: Some — ah — useful activity? Involving some general security? Like that?

PECDOV: Maybe. One of them will take over, but who? Everything is in the whirlwind. Anything can happen. Even a revolution, a real one this time. Zhdanov always said Anna Akhmatova was a traitor. Now she is writing an invisible poem about prisons and old women with endings that make people weep. What could it mean?

RUDINSKY: My God, another revolution?

PECDOV: Maybe. Maybe. Does the son know about her poems?

RUDINSKY: He knows she writes about him. But he doesn't know what.

PECDOV: Does he still hate his mother?

RUDINSKY: Well, some. She farmed him out to his grandmother. She was a poet instead of a mother. He remembers her with bitterness. I did get that out of him.

PECDOV: Did you tell him Stalin is dead?

RUDINSKY: Yesterday. He won't talk to me at all now.

PECDOV: Did he believe something would happen upon the death of Stalin?

RUDINSKY: I think so.

PECDOV: Did he say anything about any specific poem? With something overwhelming at the end of it?

RUDINSKY: No.

[*Long pause.*]

PECDOV: Ah! Damn!

RUDINSKY: I did the best I could. With my hands tied behind my back!

PECDOV: I know that. Wait outside.

[PECDOV *shakes hands with* RUDINSKY, *claps him on the back. Exit* RU-DINSKY. *Blackout. Light up on* PECDOV *and* KLARINA, *a well dressed woman in her forties. She is fierce and intelligent. She suffers from many psychological wounds.*]

PECDOV: And the title of it, evidently, is "Requiem." What I need to find out is what happens at the end of it.

KLARINA: [*Paces.*] And you think *I* can find out?

PECDOV: You of all people. Do you understand why?

KLARINA: Because she loved me, and doesn't know what I did to her.

PECDOV: [*Smiles.*] Yes. Anna Andreyevna was so popular. The plainest people loved her steamy little verses, and I'll admit it, her. Stalin is dead. I want you to put those two things together? Can you?

KLARINA: No.

PECDOV: My dear woman, our great, vast, enormous land, our Soviet Russia, never had a revolution. Not a real one. Powers shifted. The backbone similarities between our government and the Russia of the Tsars are too obvious to need comment. We changed, yes, but not like France, or America. The thought of a truly popular revolution in our colossal country is not to be endured. Those who might bring it about must be dealt with. Now Stalin is gone. The one man who made a real revolution unthinkable is dead. And it is thinkable now. [*He stares at her.*] Are you all right?

KLARINA: Yes, thank you. I just have a bit of a headache, is all.

PECDOV: Four popular artists. Friends. Mandelstam, Marina Tsvetaeva, Pasternak, Akhmatova. Only she survived. Why?

KLARINA: She is a great poet.

PECDOV: Of a sort, maybe.

KLARINA: People *love* the poems. Half Russia recites Akhmatova.

PECDOV: Good. Defend her.

KLARINA: She refused to emigrate. She wrote passionately about staying with her country. She wrote a war poem praising Stalin.

PECDOV: All right. Mandelstam, labor camp. Tsvetaeva, suicide. Pasternak, muzzled. But Akhmatova remains, cooking up some deadly
invisible opus called Requiem, of *what*, we may well ask! Do you
follow me?

KLARINA: A revolution *after* after Stalin? That's very doubtful. We
loved Stalin. Didn't we?

PECDOV: [*Quickly*.]Of course we did! But a group begins now. Es-
tablishes something. Keeps on. In a year, five? I want you to talk to
her again.

KLARINA: [*Paces*.] You can't ask me to do that.

PECDOV: Why not?

KLARINA: When she stood outside the prison walls, in those awful
lines, she had time to think. She knows it was somebody's idea.

PECDOV: Which worked very well.

KLARINA: Do you know why I did that to her?

PECDOV: You love your country.

KLARINA: Yes, but something else.

PECDOV: She took a man away from you?

KLARINA: She is Dante!

PECDOV: And you are a Russian patriot. That's better than being
Dante. You will try again. Right now.

KLARINA: She's *here*?

PECDOV: In the next room. Waiting, she thinks, to see her son.

KLARINA: Oh my God.

PECDOV: When she comes in, she will find you here instead. Her friend who put him away in the first place. Elegant.

KLARINA: What do you have to know?

PECDOV: The old woman. That ending. Listen. Troops surround Moscow this instant. Tanks at every crossroad. This city is sealed off, but by an army ready to do God knows what under orders from God knows who!

KLARINA: Remember, she had a husband shot! She has a son in chains!

PECDOV: Oh yes, I know that. If Russia faces chaos, who cares? Here, smoke. If you get nowhere, don't worry. I'll be listening. [*Exit* PEC-DOV.]

[*Blackout. Lights up on* ANNA AKHMATOVA. *She has just entered the room. She is staring, stricken, at* KLARINA. *She sinks into a chair. She is a middle aged woman, once a slim, imperious beauty, now growing pleasantly fat. She is a little unkempt, but erect, and self possessed. For many, she is the greatest poet in Russia.*]

ANNA: Oh.

[*She sits in the chair, devastated.* KLARINA *moves to the other chair, sits by her.*]

KLARINA: This is cruel.

ANNA: Yes.

KLARINA: I didn't send for you.

ANNA: I believe you.

KLARINA: I don't know where he is, or what is happening to him. Have you heard anything?

ANNA: Not in three years.

KLARINA: You're looking very —

ANNA: Thanks to you!

[*Pause.*]

KLARINA: Anna! [*Pause.*] You've known, all this time?

[*Anna nods.*]

KLARINA: It wasn't just me, you know! It was the obvious thing to do to you. Stalin had so much trouble with his own son, when it was suggested to him, he said it was the perfect solution.

ANNA: He was right. You were right. It was.

[*Pause.*]

KLARINA: Well. What are you writing now?

ANNA: Poetry in praise of Stalin.

KLARINA: I mean, anything else?

ANNA: Nothing else.

KLARINA: [*Paces.*] Just tell me, please? It's what they have to know! What else can I do but ask you, my darling?

ANNA: Nothing.

KLARINA: So tell me!

ANNA: Nothing. I've written nothing.

KLARINA: They know about Requiem.

ANNA: About what?

KLARINA: The old woman standing in line at the prisons. You are writing a poem about her, and it is considered possibly dangerous.

ANNA: An old woman in a prison line, dangerous?

KLARINA: If the old woman is created by Anna Akhmatova, yes!

ANNA: Interesting, as always, how your minds work.

KLARINA: It is your mind and how *it* works, Anna Andreyevna, they are worrying about!

ANNA: You are still beautiful.

KLARINA: What's in the poem?

ANNA: A boy once killed himself for us.

KLARINA: What overwhelming thing happens at the end of that poem?

ANNA: We drove men crazy.

KLARINA: I am very sorry to tell you that I am not the only one of your friends from the past to betray you! Others have too!

ANNA: Most. The day Zhdanov attacked me, I hadn't read the papers. I slept in, went to market. I bought my fish, wrapped in a newspaper. I went home, unwrapped my fish. Newspaper, article, Zhdanov. Death to the poet. My son in prison again. I thought it was you then.

KLARINA: God, my head!

[*Enter* MARYA.]

MARYA: Good afternoon.

KLARINA: You, too?

MARYA: Yes. You're getting nowhere. But stay.

[*They sit in the chairs downstage, facing* ANNA.]

How are you, Anna Andreyevna?

ANNA: Well, thank you.

MARYA: I wish I was.

ANNA: So do I.

MARYA: Has Klarina told you what I've done?

KLARINA: No.

MARYA: I told them what I knew about Requiem.

ANNA: Oh.

MARYA: You can imagine why.

ANNA: Yes.

MARYA: It was a boy.

ANNA: So I heard.

MARYA: They can do to my son what they did to yours. Or worse.

ANNA: Yes.

MARYA: So I told them my five words.

ANNA: I see.

MARYA: They think it's the old way of passing poetry on, but different, somehow, and worse.

ANNA: I see.

KLARINA: They think it is dangerous.

MARYA: They're afraid you are writing about something to come after the death of Stalin.

KLARINA: What happens at the end of Requiem, Anna?

KLARINA: That's what they have to know!

MARYA: They'll take it out of you, when they want to!

KLARINA: They believe us when we say we don't know what happens!

MARYA: But that can change!

KLARINA: You know we *don't* know!

MARYA: We could die!

KLARINA: If they don't find out!

MARYA: It's only a poem!

KLARINA: They can shoot us all!

MARYA: Your son! Mine!

KLARINA: You have to tell us, Anna!

MARYA: You have to tell us something!

[*Pause.*]

ANNA: I will tell you this. If you love Russia, you can dig for her.

MARYA: What?

KLARINA: Dig? For something buried?

KLARINA & MARYA: Where?

ANNA: In Petersburg. Where Mandelstam said it was.

KLARINA: Mandelstam?

MARYA: Petersburg?

ANNA: I'm tired now. We had many good times, the three of us. When you were little, Marya, and Klarina loved the voice of God. No more.

KLARINA: The voice of God?

ANNA: That's what poetry is. You've forgotten. Goodbye. [*She closes her eyes.*]

KLARINA: Anna.

MARYA: Anna.

KLARINA & MARYA: Anna!

[*Pause.* ANNA *seems to be asleep. Enter* RUDINSKY.]

RUDINSKY: I'll wake her up. [*He slams a chair down directly in front of* ANNA, *and sits in it.*] I have been living with your son. In the same cell. He isn't where you think he is. He is here. In Moscow. Maybe five blocks from here. Look at me.

[ANNA *keeps her eyes shut.*]

I can get to him in an hour. I can tell him things. Imagine.

[RUDINSKY *gets up, speaks directly into her ear.*]

He is going free. He will rot in a camp 'til he dies. His mother has used him to write a poem, for which he can be shot!

[ANNA *opens her eyes.*]

ANNA: Five blocks?

RUDINSKY: Five blocks. [*Satisfied, he sits down again.*] You've been playing games with your son's life.

ANNA: Games? Do you think, after all these years, waiting to see him again, I would refuse to tell you anything on earth? You silenced me as no other human being who ever lived. Tell me I can see him, and I will tell you anything you ask me.

RUDINSKY: What happens to the old woman? What happens at the end of the poem? *That's* what you can tell us!

ANNA: All right, but do I see my son?

RUDINSKY: I can't promise, but yes, probably!

MARYA: Anna, you gave me rain, a cow, boats and a statue. Is it the statue? Of someone — revolutionary?

ANNA: If I tell you, will that set him free?

RUDINSKY: It might!

KLARINA: Tell us, Anna!

MARYA: Please, Anna!

[*Enter* PECDOV. *He carries a decanter of brandy and two glasses.*]

PECDOV: "We will meet in Petersburg, around the grave where we buried the sun." She'll tell me now. Out.

[*Exeunt* MARYA, KLARINA *and* RUDINSKY. PECDOV *takes the chair* RUDINSKY *had set in front of* ANNA *and puts it back in place. He pours a brandy and hands it to her.*]

Brandy?

ANNA: Thank you.

[PECDOV *pours himself a brandy.*]

PECDOV: To a statue buried in the tomb of the sun. To your good health.

ANNA: To yours.

[*They sip the brandy.*]

PECDOV: So. Here we are.

ANNA: You've done very well.

PECDOV: Yes, I have. The faithful disciple. Who sat at the feet of the master poets, with such humility. Such devotion to the great causes, until I discovered the great causes were the great egos of the great poets. Skillful parasites, just like Plato says, feeding on the state. So I became a Minister of the People, and slept well at night.

ANNA: I am glad you sleep well at night.

PECDOV: Let us go back to Petersburg. To the grave of the sun.

ANNA: All right.

PECDOV: I remember it, too. Better than you, perhaps. [PECDOV *closes his eyes and recites, broadly, in the Russian manner.*] "We will meet in Petersburg, around the grave where we buried the sun —

[ANNA *closes her eyes, and recites.*]

ANNA: "And then together we will say it for the first time, the wonderful word meaning nothing —

[*Both, eyes closed, recite.*]

PECDOV: [*Reciting.*] "In the new Russian night, soft and beautiful darkness, a black velvet nowhere, the beloved eyes of sacred women are still singing, flowers blossom that will live forever —

ANNA: [*Reciting.*] "The city gathers itself like a lost cat, soldiers are stationed on the bridges, one automobile dashes blindly by, siren whooping like a screaming bird —

PECDOV: [*Reciting.*] "Tonight I will not carry my credentials, I have no fear of the soldiers. I will pray in the new Russian night, for the wonderful word meaning nothing —

ANNA: [*Reciting.*] "For fun we will stand by a fire, maybe time will fall apart, and the beloved hands of sacred women will sweep the ashes back together —

PECDOV: [*Reciting.*] "Don't worry when the candles all snuff out, in the soft and beautiful darkness, the black nowhere. The bent shoulders of sacred women are still singing—

PECDOV & ANNA: [*Reciting.*] You will not see the sun, still burning in the night."

[*Pause.*]

PECDOV: Mandelstam.

ANNA: Mandelstam.

PECDOV: And poetry, the voice of God. Do you know how he died?

ANNA: No.

PECDOV: He died paranoid in a camp, certain his filthy grub was being poisoned. He tried to stay alive by stealing food from other prisoners. They beat him to death. Great poet of the Russian land.

ANNA: I am not surprised.

PECDOV: I denounced him to Stalin.

ANNA: I am not surprised.

PECDOV: He read ten of us a poem about Stalin, in which Stalin had cockroach eyebrows, and greasy fingers staining the pages of books by men he would kill. It was the single denunciation of Stalin ever written down by anyone, and that one poem did it. Now it is your turn. But you are different. Not as a poet. As a mother.

ANNA: How ingenious, the Devil. Killing a woman with her son. Mephistopheles, blush.

PECDOV: I always forget the Christian part of you. The nun within the whore. Never mind Mephistopheles. While Stalin lived, your son was safe. Kept in prison, used to torment you, but not to be killed. Now Stalin is gone, and others will make that decision. Who is the statue that makes people weep?

[ANNA *doesn't answer.*]

I can let him go. You can be drinking champagne with him in half an hour. Or he can be shot. Not another second. Is there a statue?

ANNA: Yes.

[PECDOV *gets up.*]

PECDOV: Of someone revolutionary?

ANNA: Yes.

PECDOV: Making Russia weep?

ANNA: Yes.

PECDOV: Who?

ANNA: I am the statue.

PECDOV: What?

ANNA: I stand in front of that prison. My metal eyes weep tears. In my poem, I am the statue.

PECDOV: I don't understand.

ANNA: Of course not.

PECDOV: You have built a statue to *yourself*?

ANNA: Yes.

[*Pause.* PECDOV *laughs, richly and loudly, sits.*]

PECDOV: Made yourself a monument? Made yourself *an icon*?

ANNA: [*To him, explaining it.*] I have made a statue of an old woman, standing in a line outside a prison, waiting every day to see her son. In the line are many other women, with sons, daughters, husbands, sisters, mothers and fathers. All in prison. And to my country I say, if in some future year, you mark my life with a statue, I consent to that honor. But I will not stand in the gardens of my love affairs, or in the company of the splendid artists I have known, or before the applauding crowds who loved me, but there, in a line of women, by the riverboats and the doves, before an iron gate, which was never, not once, opened to me. Russia can remember me there, if she pleases.

PECDOV: My God! All this fuss! Anna Andreyevna, you are not a dangerous revolutionary. You are a crazy old woman.

ANNA: And you are an insect of a single day.

[*A long pause.*]

PECDOV: It's not his fault your son has a madwoman for a mother. If I make an issue of this, I'll put myself up for ridicule. Keep your mouth shut and go in peace.

ANNA: Will I ever see him again?

PECDOV: Soon, maybe. Stalin is dead, who knows what will happen. Never, maybe. Stalin is dead, who knows what will happen. Goodbye.

[ANNA *nods and starts to exit.*]

Certainly —

[ANNA *stops.*]

Statues will be made. But not of you. Of Stalin, and in time, perhaps, of me.

[ANNA *goes to him. He looks at her.*]

ANNA: Perhaps.

[*Exit* ANNA. PECDOV *stands thinking. He opens the window again. The bell tolls for Stalin. Light fades on* PECDOV, *thinking.*]

Carol K. Mack

UNPROGRAMMED
A One Act Play

UNPROGRAMMED

Carol K. Mack

Carol K. Mack, a New York playwright, is an alumna of New Dramatists, a member of The Women's Project, Dramatists Guild, The League of Professional Theatre Women/N.Y., and P.E.N. Her work includes:

Borders, recipient of The Beverly Hills Theatre Guild/Julie Harris Playwright Award, selected for Prima Facie 2 at The Denver Center for the Performing Arts,1986; *Territorial Rites*, a Susan Smith Blackburn and FDG/CBS Finalist, produced at The American Place Theatre, starring Kim Hunter and Michael Gross, 1983; *Postcards* (University of Jacksonville One Act Award) produced at Ensemble Studio Theatre, New York City, 1983; *A Safe Place* (Stanley Drama Award) premiered at The Berkshire Theatre Festival in Association with the Kennedy Center, 1981; *Survival Games*, produced in the New American Play Series by The Berkshire Theatre Festival, 1980; *Esther*, produced by Lucille Lortel at The White Barn Theatre Foundation in 1976, and Off Broadway in 1977.

Two commissions by the Actors Theatre of Louisville resulted in her one acts: *Hi Tech* and *Half Time at Halcyon Days*. *The Magenta Shift*, commissioned by the "Difficult Women's Project" funded by NYSCA, won the Playwrights' Forum Award, Theatreworks, University of Colorado, 1986. *A.K.A. Marlene* and *Postcards* were produced in 1989 at the Producers' Club, New York City. All the above one acts have received hundreds of productions ranging from the Theatre of the Open Eye, New York City to Los Angeles showcases to university and community theatre productions throughout the United States and abroad.

Current plays include: *Necessary Fictions*, nominated for a 1988 Rockefeller Fellowship; *Last Resorts* (a duo of one acts); songs for a political cabaret, The Snicker Factory, 1988; *Unprogrammed*, a new one act play, performed at The Westport Theatre Artists' Lab, 1989 and selected for *Best Short Plays*, 1990.

Carol K. Mack's earlier appearance in this series was in the 1985 edition with *Half Time at Halcyon Days*, a comedy about five women in a health spa. For the past six years, Ms. Mack has taught "Life Stories," a fiction-writing class, at New York University, where she is now completing her Master of Arts degree in Religious Studies with a concentration on the traditions of the East.

CHARACTERS

George, edgy, insecure, very intelligent computer programmer.

Harold, suburban space salesman, GEORGE's drinking buddy.

Caprice, beautiful, candid, young woman. Has a subtle, unplaceable accent.

SET: *Downstage Left is a bar, with two stools upstage of it that face the audience; Upstage Center there is a small table and two chairs; Stage Right there is a rock. All the above seating areas are preset. Handprops are carried on and off by actors.*

TIME: *Summer in suburbia.*

[*Lights up.* GEORGE *and* HAROLD *lean on bartop Stage Left.* GEORGE *is cold sober and* HAROLD *is cosmically drunk.*]

GEORGE: [*Intensely.*] Harold. Listen to me, Harold. Am I your friend?

[*No response.*]

Am I your friend or am I NOT your friend?

HAROLD: What?

GEORGE: Am I or not?

HAROLD: Sure.

GEORGE: Right! Now, did I , *how* many times, how many times did I tell you, Harold?

HAROLD: Huhnh?

GEORGE: *Never,* Rule Number One, *never* do you give up *what* in a relationship?

HAROLD: What?

GEORGE: Control, Harold, control!

HAROLD: I love her, George, I love her!

GEORGE: This is what I'm *saying.* Tell me if this isn't what I'm telling you: What're you doing? You're reacting to re*act*ions! You're not even *you.* You're a chain reaction. This is what you want out of life?

HAROLD: I want Brenda back.

GEORGE: Brenda, Jesus, Harold, Brenda! You should *know* by now! We're talking offense, not defense. With Brenda, you re*act,* she walks on your face!

HAROLD: Yeah.

GEORGE: I'm trying to *help* you!

HAROLD: I see what you're saying.

GEORGE: Good.

HAROLD: But Brenda ... no listen, I can read Brenda already. Did I tell you there'd be a note when I got home? This is *what?* The third time! [*He takes nuts from bowl places them one by one on bartop.*] She loves me, she loves me not, she took the Volvo.

GEORGE: [*Eats nuts as they hit.*] You don't have to go through this, Harold. You don't have to *feel!* That should be your goal, Harold: numbness.

HAROLD: If she'd only give me one more chance I'd ... I'd be, it'd be totally different. I'd go straight home from the train.

GEORGE: Get hold of yourself.

HAROLD: I GOTTA get Brenda back.

GEORGE: You've got one chance. Did I make you an offer that could save your life, huh?

HAROLD: [*Confusedly, trying to remember.*] You know where she went?

GEORGE: NO. I told you I could put Brenda in my database and get you a printout on her every move.

HAROLD: Oh yeah! How do I do that again?

GEORGE: *I* do it! *I* do it! I'm the computer programmer. You're a space salesman, Harold, remember?

HAROLD: Oh yeah! You wanted me to tell you ...

GEORGE: Facts! Hard facts. For my database. I programmed all variables in over two million relationships. A trillion gigabytes of female behavior! I can calculate their any move. It's all in there. No woman can take us by surprise. I'll get you a printout on Brenda by morning.

[HAROLD *passes out on the floor.* GEORGE *watches his body fall with some disgust.*]

This is what happens when you're unprepared!

[GEORGE *steps over* HAROLD *and* HAROLD *remains corpse-like for the following scene.* GEORGE *begins jogging as he leaves the bar area and loops around the stage. He soon hears a voice (offstage) — a woman's voice singing a French folksong. He jogs slowly as he hears. The* WOMAN *enters singing. She is very beautiful. She sits calmly on a rock Stage Right and hums, oblivious.*]

GEORGE: [*Upon seeing the* WOMAN, *startled, to himself, flatly, while jogging.*] A Student, Undergrad, French Major, *no!* Maybe exchange student. Try Exchange Student, post grad, or an *act*ress. Possible. Possible. Retry! *Act*ress, memorizes part in . . . NO. Try Pseudo-francophile, spots ME, *genuine* Francophile jogging, NO. How would she know? But gorgeous, wow, whoa! Why so pale? Age? Age? Age? [*He slows near her, nonchalant.*] Qu'est-ce-que vous chantez, Mademoiselle?

CAPRICE: [*Full of wonder, as if awakening.*] Where am I?

GEORGE [*Nonplussed by her full direct gaze.*] You were, uh, singing something.

CAPRICE: It's *you* then . . .!

GEORGE: Right. Well, I thought I recognized the melody.

CAPRICE: [*Still delighted.*] You heard me! You heard me singing!

GEORGE: Right. That's why I asked.

CAPRICE: I don't know the name, but if you'd like I'll sing it from the beginning. It has over a hundred verses. It's about a maiden who . . .

GEORGE: It's O.K. Just thought I recognized it. I have a small collection of obscure European folk tapes.

CAPRICE: Really!

GEORGE: Some old, some new. Some C.D.'s

CAPRICE: Oh I would so love to hear them. May I come to your home?

GEORGE: [*To himself, overwhelmed.*] Careful . . . mind click. Boot *up!* Come on! . . . She could be homeless.

CAPRICE: What?

GEORGE: You're not from around here, huh?

CAPRICE: No, are you?

GEORGE: [*Sotto voce.*] Toulouse. No. Try Canada. Not Connecticut. Not Connecticut.

CAPRICE: [*Smiling delightedly as if at a toy.*] What did you say? You have such a nice whisper.

GEORGE: My name's George Appleman. I'm in computers.

CAPRICE: Nice to meet you George. *Very* nice. [*Shakes hands, moving closer.*] My name is Caprice.

GEORGE: [*Backs off.*] Uh, you just get to town?

CAPRICE: Yes!

GEORGE: You a . . . *dancer!* You look like a dancer! Am I right?

CAPRICE: Uh, yes. I do dance.

GEORGE: Bingo! Caprice what?

CAPRICE: What?

GEORGE: You have a last name?

CAPRICE: Just Caprice.

GEORGE: [*To himself.*] Stage name. Getting there. Chill out. Take your time, George. [*To her, suddenly avuncular.*] Look, I don't know how it is where you come from but here, I mean, *I'm* O.K., but do yourself a favor, don't talk to just any guy who . . . I mean there are a lot of creeps around.

CAPRICE: Oh . . . but you're O.K.?

GEORGE: Yeah, sure. I'm O.K.!

CAPRICE: Then would you help me to find my way?

GEORGE: [*Helpless from direct appeal. His eyes dart from side to side.*] Some remake of Candid Camera. Sure! Maybe Letterman? No, then *what?* A hidden camera someplace. GOTta be. Keep smiling. Practical joke. [*Smiles in all directions for camera.*]

CAPRICE: George? You're O.K.?

GEORGE: [*"Cheerfully" suave for camera.*] Sure. No problem. Where to?

CAPRICE: [*Hands him slip of paper.*] Here is where I will live.

GEORGE: [*Stares at paper.*] Not far from me. I jog along there sometimes just to look . . . very pretty neighborhood. [*Embarrassed at revealing anything.*] Is it a sublet or . . .

CAPRICE: It has many trees?

GEORGE: Yeah. A lotta trees. Why?

CAPRICE: I was wondering.

GEORGE: [*Sotto voce.*] Why THAT? Who IS this? What accent? Au Pair? Au Pair? [*To her.*] You could walk it from here, unless you've got a car . . . ? [*She shakes her head "no."*] I'll make a little map . . .

[*She stands very very close watching. He is aware of her closeness, writes.*]

On paper you can see the layout better. Now we are "Here." Get that so far?

CAPRICE: George, excuse me . . . ?

GEORGE: What?

CAPRICE: Do you, could you, spare me a few moments to walk with me there?

GEORGE: [*Swallows as he sinks into her eyes.*] Uh, sure. Sure, why not?

[*They exit together.* HAROLD *simultaneously stands at bar, rising from the floor drink in hand.* GEORGE, *who doesn't complete the "exit," loops around jogging back to bar, speaking as he does.*]

GEORGE: What was I supposed to say, *no?* Somebody asks you for help crossing a street you say *no?* I just can't believe it.

[*Arriving at* HAROLD, *directly.*]

I meet this girl . . . no. Girl is *wrong* . . . a *wom*an, no. Woman is wrong.

HAROLD: Person?

GEORGE: Person is wrong.

HAROLD: A *what?*

GEORGE: A WHAT? I don't know! A . . . what would she *be* — with a name like that? First I think she's playing with my mind, right? She's gorgeous, and she's gotta know it. You don't walk around gorgeous and not know, you know? But she's like, *surprised* I hear her singing. The only broad on the whole road singing, right? So why's she surprised? WHY?

HAROLD: You better have a drink.

GEORGE: O.K., O.K. But why no last name?

HAROLD: You asked her?

GEORGE: Yeah, Caprice what? Nothing. Where you from? Too long a story. Just ... Caprice ... who's got a fantastic body and navy blue eyes! [GEORGE *collapses*.]

HAROLD: George, what's the matter?

GEORGE: I gotta find out *who* this chick is! Crack the source code! She's from ... outta nowhere, Har! Maybe a *hooker*, enter that. But No, NO, she's a *kid* and like out of some old painting, like a Botticelli ...

HAROLD: French. You said French. Not Italian.

GEORGE: It doesn't compute. She acts like she doesn't know what fork to use. Not a hick but like from Sherwood Forest, you know?

HAROLD: No ...

GEORGE: Spacey?

HAROLD: Oh. Maybe she's *on* something.

GEORGE: [*A burst of Romantic enthusiasm, a very different tone.*] There were all these little yellow butterflies, Harold. Like they all hatched at the same time and they're flying all over the road and then: there she *is* with this ... *face!*

HAROLD: You didn't tell about the butterflies.

GEORGE: They mean something? Should I enter them? WHAT?

HAROLD: How would I know.

GEORGE: What'd you say it for?

HAROLD: Sounds *weird*. A whole bunch hatching like that. This whole thing sounds real weird, George.

GEORGE: Yeah! And another thing, she's so *pale*. I figure maybe she's out on a weekend pass ... But then, she's so ... she *looks* at you. I'm talking *enormous* eye contact. Delete mental. Delete. Delete.

HAROLD: So whaddya got?

GEORGE: *Nothing* is what I've got on her ... except she doesn't know her way around and it makes you kind of want to ...

HAROLD: Watch out, George!

GEORGE: What?

HAROLD: You're in over your head with no variables. You know, re*act*ing?

GEORGE: [*Straightens tie.*] Don't worry about me. There are ways to format for aberrant behavior. I mean we are living Post Surprise, man! Post post.

HAROLD: If you say so . . .

GEORGE: With the right data everything's predictable! Halley's Comet is a *routine*, Harold. An eclipse? You don't have time for it live, you stick it on the VCR. This is an Age Beyond Reason! Thank God.

HAROLD: I see what you're saying. But this Caprice . . .

GEORGE: [*Snaps.*] What?! What about her?!

HAROLD: Why not relax and enjoy, huh? So you can't figure every move . . . makes it kind of interesting, huh?

GEORGE: Interesting! A *tarantula* is interesting! You, of all people . . .

HAROLD: [*Shrugs.*] Takes the fun out of . . .

GEORGE: Fun?! Look at the guy who lives near the volcano and *knows* when it's gonna blow. Then look at Pompei!

HAROLD: But maybe this once . . .

GEORGE: Once is all it takes. I've been moving too fast. It's all processing. Let this chick feed me hard facts. I'll take notes. She'll slip. She'll cross reference herself right into my program. Trust me, Harold, I'm at the controls.

HAROLD: But George . . . listen! . .. Brenda came home! What do I do? . . . hey?

[HAROLD, *slightly glazed, watches as* GEORGE *leaves his side, shakes his head and exits with glass, while* CAPRICE *enters from opposite side, her arms laden with flowers.* GEORGE *follows her glumly, notebook in hand.*]

CAPRICE: There are flowers everywhere you look in this town, isn't it *wonderful*, George? Even in the grocery stores where you buy the food, and they also play music.

GEORGE: [*Grimly.*] They didn't have flowers where you come from, Caprice? Or they didn't have food?

CAPRICE: [*Wide-eyed.*] What, dear?

GEORGE: [*Startled.*] Nothing. "Dear"?! [*Writes in notebook, aloud.*] Too much too soon.

CAPRICE: George, tell me again about your work. It's so *intricate*. You seem so dedicated. Always taking notes, always thinking about your work.

GEORGE: She's trying to escape!

CAPRICE: Excuse me?

GEORGE: [*A benediction.*] I want you to know, whatever you did or wherever you came from, I wouldn't hold it against you.

CAPRICE: Thank you!

GEORGE: I've heard just about everything. Nothing you could tell me would make headlines in my brain. So feel free to tell me anything at all about your past, all right?

CAPRICE: Thank you. And thank you for these beautiful flowers!

GEORGE: Anytime.

CAPRICE: We should put them in water.

GEORGE: All right then, forget the past. How about *now?* I'm not pushing but I was wondering . . . you have a job or what?

CAPRICE: You want me to "haf a job"?

GEORGE: ME? I mean hey, you're paying the rent and, I mean you said you were a dancer?

CAPRICE: I dance. Yes. I do and also I sing.

GEORGE: But what do you *eat?* I mean are you a medical illustrator or a *what?* Look, Caprice, whenever I get off the train, you're at the station. If I was some other guy I'd think you were maybe following me . . . [*Thinks, writes notes.*] Hired to tail me, but *why?* Am I in some top secret program I don't know about? Being cleared for government work . . . [*To* CAPRICE.] Are you C.I.A.?

CAPRICE: [*Laughs, delighted.*] You are such a funny man, George. . . . C.I.A. You make me laugh.

GEORGE: I do, huh?

CAPRICE: Yes. You, how do you say? Break me up. But about my job . . .

GEORGE: Yes?

CAPRICE: Could I become a computer programmer like you?

GEORGE: That's it! Count me out. I don't like this game. I'll tell you what, Caprice, I'll give you a call sometime, we'll do lunch.

CAPRICE: I think you are angry.

GEORGE: You *think* I'm angry?

CAPRICE: Because I'm interested in your work?

GEORGE: Oh please don't look at me like that!

CAPRICE: I said something wrong. I am so sorry. Don't go, George ... please! Would you like to come and stay with me? We'd have much more time to talk.

GEORGE: You mean ... uh ...

CAPRICE: Come live with me, George.

GEORGE: I ... uh ... let me think about that um option, O.K.? I'll uh get back to you. [GEORGE *stumbles to the bar, a broken man, while* CA-PRICE *exits with flowers and* HAROLD, *notably sober, in new jacket, enters and observes his friend drinking.*]

GEORGE: Data data data data dammit ... damn her. She can't have my body!

HAROLD: Hey look, if you're not interested, I'll take her number.

GEORGE: Harold, you don't get it. I move onto her turf it's over. I watch you slobbering over Brenda like some sub-neanderthal, YES, this is the difference. Outta the ooze step by step from the amoeba to *me* — no backsliding now.

HAROLD: I never met a broad with navy blue eyes. Brenda's got ... jeeze I don't know what color Brenda's eyes are, I can't believe it ...

GEORGE: [*Already in a construct.*] O.K. Who's paying the rent? A husband maybe. Ex? Traveling? Yes, enter Diplomat, which explains ... I got it: he's stationed in some remote ... but how about *her?* She's setting me up! I move in, some embassy guy shows up and ... of *course*. Third world, gotta be! She learned English as a second language and that's why she talks funny. Yes! This could be big. I could be getting sucked into *espionage*. Sure, blackmail me for my computer program for some whoa! ... I mean Harold otherwise ... I mean *look* at me. Why would she pick *me*, huh? Why ME?

HAROLD: [*Has listened with increasing alarm.*] Uh, George, what does your doctor say?

GEORGE: What?!

HAROLD: Your shrink. Did you tell him?

GEORGE: It's AUGUST, Harold. Why do you think I'm talking to you!?

HAROLD: O.K. O.K. Chill out. You want me to meet her. Just to give you a second opinion, huh?

GEORGE: [*Miserable.*] I know what you'll say. Anybody would live happily with her forever and that's where *your* head is.

HAROLD: Does she play the piano?

GEORGE: Course she plays the piano. What do you care if she plays the piano?

HAROLD: I always thought it was a nice thing . . . you know, to play the piano. Brenda plays the piano. I think her eyes are hazel.

GEORGE: Caprice plays the piano, flute, cello and lute. She speaks at least four languages and she doesn't know how to drive.

HAROLD: Now there's a lotta data right there! How come you can't find her in your program?

GEORGE: I keep getting error messages. Abort. Retry.

HAROLD: Why not just marry her?

GEORGE: That is the *sickest* advice I've ever heard! She nearly burned out my motherboard!

HAROLD: Could you let go of my tie, George? Brenda likes me very neat. She says that was a major pothole in the relationship . . . me being a slob. So you know what, George? We made these lists, see, of all our likes and hates and priorities and we're building a compatibility column. Uh, how do you like my new jacket? Brenda picked it out. Tassel loafers . . . ?

[GEORGE, *totally preoccupied has let go of* HAROLD's *tie and exits, thinking.*]

HEY, George? Where are you going? I want to explain how we're working it all out, George . . .

[*But* GEORGE *has exited and* HAROLD *follows.* CAPRICE *enters and sits at a small table Upstage with a glass in one hand, a menu in the other.* GEORGE *enters, carrying a menu. Sits, keeping a close eye on* CAPRICE. *He crosses his legs and smiles a phoney smile at her. She smiles back a genuine one.*]

CAPRICE: [*Raising her glass.*] To us!

GEORGE: [*Raises glass, clinks, tightly.*] I found this restaurant last winter. Very understated. Food is remarkable. Food people haven't found it yet. When they do, you won't be able to get in the door.

CAPRICE: I *love* it here!

GEORGE: You *do?*

CAPRICE: Oh yes!

GEORGE: [*Not too sure.*] Well what it lacks in ambience, it makes up for in the paté.

CAPRICE: Oh, George, you *know* so much!

GEORGE: Not enough.

CAPRICE: And you're so modest.

GEORGE: Caprice, there's something I want to discuss with you.

CAPRICE: Yes?

GEORGE: I've known you for almost, what, three months? And I don't know the first thing about you.

CAPRICE: But I . . . I am just, myself.

GEORGE: Oh, no, you're not!

CAPRICE: I'm not?

GEORGE: No. You change all the time. Like whenever I think you're gonna say one thing you say something else. And also I don't be-lieve anybody can be happy all the time. Why are you always happy!?

CAPRICE: Oh, George, have I done something to make you unhappy?

GEORGE: You've made me very happy, Caprice. You make me ecstat-ically happy. But I don't know *why.*

CAPRICE: Oh?

GEORGE: So you see, this relationship needs *work.*

CAPRICE: So you . . . won't just let us *be,* George?

GEORGE: I think it's perfectly *normal* for me to be a little curious about your childhood, your roots, other men in your life.

CAPRICE: [*Clear as water.*] There is no other man in my life.

GEORGE: *Before,* Caprice.

CAPRICE: I'm afraid for us. I must warn you that . . . if you can't ac-cept me now, you won't accept my origin.

GEORGE: Anything. Tell me anything!

CAPRICE: [*Sips wine, looks at him.*] George . . . ?

GEORGE: Trust me.

CAPRICE: Well, in a sense, I'm . . . only an illusion.

GEORGE: Then let's have the truth.

CAPRICE: That's what I'm saying, George. I am, in a sense, a figment of your imagination.

GEORGE: That your first drink?

CAPRICE: I'm sorry, George. I am . . . like the reach of your mind to, uh, the other side . . . like "word-wrap," George. [*Pause.*] I'm the parts that fell out of your database. The perfect parts.

[*Long pause.*]

GEORGE: [*Quietly nods.*] I know that *you* know that my analyst is away and I'm without support . . .

CAPRICE: I'm so sorry George. I have no power to change your mind . . . I'm only *part* of it.

GEORGE: Did you order that wine from the waiter over there?

CAPRICE: Yes?

GEORGE: So that guy sees you too, huh?

CAPRICE: [*Nods, simply.*] Because you do.

GEORGE: [*Nods.*]That's good, that's very good.

CAPRICE: [*Hopefully.*] But all you have to do is believe in me. Is that so much to ask?

GEORGE: Now she's quoting Tinkerbell!

CAPRICE: I thought that you'd never accept it.

GEORGE: All I wanted was the regular stuff. Where you went to school, your last name, where you were born, single, married, divorced, who you voted for in the last election, nothing personal, hobbies. And what do I get? This FANTASY!

CAPRICE: I wish I could tell you what you want but . . . um . . . I was never here before so I didn't get to vote.

GEORGE: Right. Keep it up. You realize I don't remember my dreams. I've never had a daydream.

CAPRICE: Don't blame me, George, I was born for you.

GEORGE: I deal exclusively with reality chips.

CAPRICE: You heard me singing!

GEORGE: You're telling me I hallucinate daily and at the same time function brilliantly as a computer programmer. Give me a break, babe.

CAPRICE: I don't know how all these invisible forces operate, but I am sure there's a logic to them, if that makes you feel better. I suppose *some* part of your mind must have wanted . . . something you couldn't program.

GEORGE: Have you ever spent a real long time in any kind of institution?

CAPRICE: [*Last shot.*] I'm telling you the truth! You're my destiny. My beginning. My end. I exist only so long as you believe in me.

GEORGE: It's original. Not a line you hear much around here. Brigadoon maybe. Not here! I have to hand it to you. [*Stands.*] I'd like you to see my shrink if he ever gets back from Hawaii. I'm going to write his name and number here for you. [*Writes while speaking.*] Meanwhile, it's better for both of us, assuming there *are* two of us — we just, don't see each other for a while.

CAPRICE: Oh . . .

GEORGE: It won't work. I can't go along with this creation myth of yours. Tell me you're a channel, maybe I'd buy it, but this — this is too much. I don't want to hurt you but . . . [*Lights flash.*] I don't believe in you babe, O.K.? I've said it!

[GEORGE *is startled;* CAPRICE *isn't there.*]

Caprice!?

[*Immediately* GEORGE, *in shock, heads to the bar area.* HAROLD, *enters area with glass in hand, meets him there. As if electrified.*]

Before the PATÉ, Har! Not a sound, nothing. *Gone!*

HAROLD: Like Brenda.

GEORGE: She leaves notes. She doesn't vanish.

HAROLD: So she walked fast. She was pissed off.

GEORGE: Yeah? . . . Listen to this, Harold. I wait a couple of days. No calls. I call. No answer. I go by her house . . . all right. Say what you want, but Harold, it's gone. There's this construction pit and the foundation's in already.

HAROLD: They work fast. You know my view? That fantastic view I'm paying for in blood? Last Sunday I pull the shade up, half a condo is smack in the view. What're you gonna do?

GEORGE: She *vanished*, O.K.? I'm not gonna delude myself. I'm gonna *commit* myself. Should I commit myself, Harold, huh?

HAROLD: Over some broad? This is like an allergic reaction — get it together.

GEORGE: It's all over. I'm a failed system.

HAROLD: You're overreacting. Look at me. Have you happened to notice what I'm drinking? Perrier. And here's the good news. Toast: George I want you to be the godfather!

GEORGE: Congratulations. I better tell you something first.

HAROLD: Yeah?

GEORGE: [*Drinks in one shot.*] You may not want me.

HAROLD: You didn't kill her, did you George? What'd you do — bury her in this construction pit?

GEORGE: I didn't *do* anything. [*Looks around nervously.*] It's what I *saw*. This morning. See I . . . I'm trying to jog again. Work up my endorphins. Get over *her*, whatever she was . . . so I'm jogging, I'm sweating, I'm breathing hard and suddenly all these yellow butterflies . . .

HAROLD: The butterflies!

GEORGE: Why do you keep harping on them!

HAROLD: They sound like killer bees. Sci fi. You should carry bug spray.

GEORGE: [*Nods dreamily.*] A cloud of them. Same spot. Same road. Same time. I look up and expect to see Caprice . . . like maybe she's got a box of butterflies she lets out, like magicians with the pigeons.

HAROLD: A box of butterflies?

GEORGE: [*Carried away into his thought.*] I'm thinking PLEASE, please give me one more chance! I won't question. I'll just *accept*!

HAROLD: Yeah, and?

GEORGE: This is gonna sound a lot worse than it is, Harold . . . there's this, well, it looks *almost* like a regular white horse standing on top of the hill looking at me. But it's not a horse, Harold. It's a centaur.

HAROLD: A senator!?

GEORGE: No. A . . . half horse, half man . . . not in a bush or anything. Right out there! I figure it could've come from some stable, only it's not a horse. It's a centaur.

HAROLD: [*Snaps his fingers.*] They're shooting a Greek film!

GEORGE: I look for the cameras, the crew. Nothing. I'm being honest with you Harold, I even thought my reflector glasses were defective. But when I take them off the thing's still there and it's looking at *me*! [*Pause.*]

HAROLD: Yeah, well, George, I'd like to help you out here, but I can't afford to get involved with this level of fantasy. I just got my life together. I'm having the house painted . . . we have crabgrass and uh, other problems — priorities. *You* understand.

GEORGE: [*Grabs* HAROLD's *sleeve, desperate.*] Why ME, Har? Why would these imaginary things . . . why would they single me out like this?! First *her*, then some mythical *beast* — it's like a *conspiracy*!

HAROLD: [*Slowly, humoring him.*] Who could be behind it, you think?

GEORGE: [*Crazed.*] Like a competitor maybe trying to drive me over the edge . . . *motive*: I'm thinking what if one of the chicks on the database figures I'm developing an ultimate gender weapon and she gets together with other chicks . . . to them my program could wipe them out. Enter that!

HAROLD: So you think there's some large Feminist Consortium behind it.

GEORGE: Who else? Who'd want to drive me crazy?! I know women with the means and the motive, why not, why not?

HAROLD: [*Straightening out his sleeve.*] I don't know, George, it's not my field. I'm a space salesman, remember?

GEORGE: Who do I look like? Merlin!?

HAROLD: Look . . .

GEORGE: [*Pulling himself together.*] I'm a scientist, a complete empiricist, I don't touch this stuff.

HAROLD: That's better, man!

GEORGE: You've known me how long? Did I ever once interface with anything metaphysical?! Forget it!

HAROLD: Good, good. Whew . . . I thought for a minute there you . . .

GEORGE: [*Evenly.*] No I'm fine. I'm fine. I'm perfectly fine.

HAROLD: Great. [*Beat.*]

GEORGE: So you know what I told it, Harold?

HAROLD: Not the centaur?

GEORGE: The, *yeah*, the thing with the half and half, yeah.

HAROLD: [*Carefully.*] No, George, what did you tell it?

GEORGE: [*Pleased, calmly, completely insane.*] I said: go find some *crackpot* that believes in you! Find some jerk out there, I'm not your man! This is the *wrong* century and the *wrong* season. You're out of *season*! That's what I told it. It's AUGUST!

[HAROLD *exits.*]

Where are you going Harold? I *told* it I didn't believe in it. What would *you* have said? Harold, I'm your best friend, I taught you everything you know . . . Harold?

[*BLACKOUT.*]

Richard Nelson

THE CHERRY ORCHARD

CHERRY ORCHARD

Richard Nelson

Richard Nelson's stage plays include *Some Americans Abroad* (Royal Shakespeare Company, Lincoln Center Theatre Company, New York), *Principia Scriptoriae* (RSC, Manhattan Theatre Club, New York), *Between East and West* (Hampstead), as well as *The Vienna Notes*, *Rip Van Winkle or the Works*, *An American Comedy*, and *The Return of Pinnochio* which have been produced by many theatres in the United States. He is the author of numerous adaptations and translations which have been seen at theatres across the United States and on Broadway, and he wrote the book for the Broadway production of the musical, *Chess*. Richard Nelson has won many awards, including two Obies, a 1987 *Time Out* Award, a Guggenheim Fellowship and the 1986 ABC Television Playwriting Award. His television plays include *Sensibility and Sense* and *The Ending of a Sentence* (both American Playhouse, Public TV, United States). *Two Shakespearean Actors* was performed by the RSC in the Swan Theatre, Stratford in September, 1990.

PROJECTION
1986
THE CHERRY ORCHARD

SCENE: *A room in a house that has been closed up; a few chairs, with dust covers.* LIBBY, *her brother,* FRANK, *and his wife,* JUDITH *sit and wait.*

[*Pause.*]

LIBBY: Have you been watching the Irangate hearings?

[FRANK *shakes his head.*]

Neither have I.

FRANK: What a ridiculous name.

[*Short pause.*]

JUDITH: I watched a little. I couldn't take more. You watch and end up asking yourself — . Well — . [*She looks at* FRANK.] I don't know. [*Beat.*] Why *do* we have to tear everything down? We're just not happy unless we're destroying, are we?

FRANK: No, I don't think we are. [*Beat.*] Though not everyone anymore. I wouldn't include everyone.

[JUDITH *nods. Short pause. To* LIBBY.] By the way I brought different color stickers. We each take a color, you, Tom and me, and mark what furniture we might each want to keep. Then, I guess, we sort of horse trade. [*He laughs.*] There's a book about dividing things up. About estates. They have a lot of great suggestions like that. [*Short pause.*] We could start —

LIBBY: Wait for Tom, he'll be off soon.

[*Short pause.*]

JUDITH: Odd, sitting here without your mother. She'd never have let any of you three kids sit like this here, without her being a part of it.

LIBBY: She still is a part of it. She is the reason for it.

JUDITH: Of course, I didn't mean —

FRANK: Judy meant, Libby, that Mom would have really enjoyed this. All of us together; sitting around her living room. [*Beat.*] She missed that. She always told me on the phone how much she missed that. [*Beat.*] But of course she's here in spirit. [*To* JUDITH.] And that's all Libby meant.

[*Short pause.*]

LIBBY: [*To* JUDITH.] I don't think I've thanked you for your note. I was very touched.

FRANK: She writes wonderful notes, doesn't she?

LIBBY: If this was any indication —

FRANK: The one she wrote to Tom, you could publish it, I think.

JUDITH: Frank —

FRANK: I'm serious. [*Beat.*] Take a compliment. Libby was complimenting you.

[*Short pause.*]

JUDITH: I figured that since because of the kids, I couldn't come right away, with Frank, then at least — Well — [*She looks at* FRANK.] I wanted you to know that my thoughts were with you.

LIBBY: You made that clear, thank you.

JUDITH: I felt badly; if Pete hadn't just been getting over the —

LIBBY: Judy, please, you do not owe anyone an apology.

FRANK: That's what I told her too, Libby. Judy, come on now, just forget it. [*Beat.*] We're all here now. [*Beat.*] We all were at the funeral.

[TOM, LIBBY *and* FRANK's *younger brother, enters.*]

TOM: That was Taylor. [*Beat; he sits.*] He'll take the case. I told you Frank we'd get someone.

FRANK: As I said, I don't think we should —

TOM: Let me finish. He'll split what we win, so we pay him nothing. That *was* your concern, Frank, that we pay him nothing.

FRANK: [*To himself.*] Shit.

JUDITH: [*Trying to calm him.*] Frank —

FRANK: Where did he get this guy?

TOM: *You* said if we paid him nothing.

FRANK: But there is no case! I'm a doctor, Tom, there's no grounds here for malpractice. What kind of shit lawyer —

TOM: You went to high school with Taylor —

FRANK: From what I remember about the high school in this town that is not a recommendation. [*Beat. To* LIBBY.] He's found an ambulance chaser. We're supposed to put ourselves through hell —

TOM: [*To* LIBBY.] He's president of the Optimists Club. You've seen him. He's very well known in this town.

LIBBY: Taylor? What's his first name?

TOM: George. I think George.

FRANK: [*To* LIBBY.] When I said, okay as long as it doesn't cost us anything, the estate anything — I also meant the emotional cost. Do you know, Libby, what the emotional cost of something like this can be? Do you have any idea?

JUDITH: [*To* LIBBY.] A friend of Frank's was sued for malpractice. He'd done nothing. His wife, just her, lost about forty pounds; she was down to nothing —

TOM: I don't care about the doctor, Judith!!

FRANK: [*Yells.*] Don't shout!! [*Beat.*] Look, if all we're going to do is shout —

TOM: Look. It's not the money. I don't care about that. We can give that away. Flush it down the toilet.

FRANK: [*To* LIBBY.] An intelligent comment. Tom always did have a peculiar way of managing his money, didn't he?

TOM: [*To* JUDITH.] But come on listen to me, she goes in for a physical from this guy, he says he can find nothing wrong — This is a complete physical, or at least that's what she paid for —

JUDITH: I know all this, Tom.

TOM: [*Ignoring her.*] And within four weeks, she's falling down steps, and she's got a tumor the size of a —

FRANK: That can happen!

TOM: Then we'll see in court, won't we? Taylor has no qualms about taking this all the way to —

FRANK: [*To* LIBBY.] He's not going to get me sitting in a courtroom.

LIBBY: If you're talking to Tom, talk *to* him.

FRANK: [*To* LIBBY.] I'm not going to listen to lawyers pick over an autopsy report of my mother!

TOM: You don't have to do shit, Frank. Fly back to Phoenix. Forget about everything. Forget about us. [*Beat.*] Leave us in peace.

LIBBY: Tom —

TOM: I'll drive you to the airport. When do you want to go?! [*Beat.*] Just say when.

[*Short pause.*]

JUDITH: Our flight isn't for another four hours.

TOM: They've got a nice lounge there you could wait in. If that's what you want to do.

[*Pause.*]

FRANK: She was my Mother too, Tom, you're not the only one who's upset.

[*Pause.*]

JUDITH: [*Getting up.*] Maybe your Mother left some coffee. [*Beat.*] Of course there won't be any milk . . . [*She goes.*]

[*Pause.*]

FRANK: [*Gets up and walks around.*] Why? Why do we always look for someone or something to blame? I guess that's just human nature, right? I do understand, Tom, I really do.

[TOM *laughs.*]

What? What is humorous about that? [*Pause.*] The facts are: our mother has died. And a malpractice suit is not going to bring her back, pal. I know that. [*Beat.*] Libby knows that.

LIBBY: Speak for yourself, Frank.

FRANK: So speak, then. [*Short pause. He shrugs and continues.*] Such a suit, I promise you, will only cause us all considerable pain. And for what? You've said it's not the money. So it must be to get even. Is vengeance what you're after, Tom?

TOM: [*To* LIBBY.] Taylor also said that since Mom smoked throughout the fifties, he'd try to get her name on a class action against the tobacco companies. [*Beat.*] They say it's only time before one of those is won. The tide seems to be turning, he says.

FRANK: Fuck!!! [*Short pause.*] Will you ever grow up, boy? [*Beat.*] So it has to be multi-nationals that killed our Mom. It's big business; so that's the murderer! Pretty soon, you're going to end up blaming President Reagan! Don't you see how pathetic you've become, Tommy?!! [*Beat.*] Get off your high horse, and you'll see that this country is not as awful as you think. [*Beat.*] But then again, I don't delude myself for a second that I can convince you of this. [*Beat.*] So let's just say we see the world a little differently.

TOM: No argument there.

[*Short pause.*]

FRANK: And as I said, she is my Mom too. So you can tell your shit lawyer to kiss off. [*Pause.*] Hey look, when I walked into this house, ask Judith, I must have turned as white as a sheet. I don't want time to pass by either. I don't want people I love to die. But they do. It does. It has. [*Beat. Laughs to himself.*] Having kids, you really get to see the time go by. I'm really sorry you both —. But there's still time. Mom loved grandkids, you know. [*Beat.*] She doted on Pete. I'd say if we really cared about doing something for Mom —

LIBBY: Shut up, Frank. [*Beat.*] You want a family. Fine. Fine. But just shut up. [*Long pause.*] We have things we have to get done. Right? Frank and Judy have a plane to catch. [*Beat.*] Here, I've written the thank-you notes; I thought it'd be nice if we all signed; that's how Mom always made us do it. [*Beat.*] Even when she wrote our thank-you notes herself.

TOM: [*Smiling.*] So you're Mom now? [*Beat.*] I wouldn't object.

FRANK: Give me a stack, I'll sign. [*Beat.*] You should be thanked for thinking of this, Libby. Thank-you notes never entered my mind.

LIBBY: Your wife reminded me.

[*Pause as they begin to sign.*]

TOM: Does it matter who signs first? Should I leave aspace?

LIBBY: No. No it doesn't matter.

[*Short pause.*]

FRANK: [*Looking at one card.*] The O'Hara's flowers I thought were especially beautiful. Maybe I should say that.

LIBBY: I did. [*Beat.*] Did you read my note? Both of you are just signing your names without reading my notes? How do you know what the hell I've said?

FRANK: [*Trying to make a joke.*] God Tommy, Mom makes us not only sign our names but we have to read what she writes too. [*He laughs; no one else does.*]

TOM: Flowers. Mom I'm sure would rather have had the money go to —

FRANK: Mom loved cut flowers.

TOM: I didn't say she didn't. [*Beat.*] When Dad died, we asked people to give donations to somewhere.

FRANK: That was you idea, not hers. One more thing you shoved down our throats.

TOM: Not true. You know that isn't true.

FRANK: [*Ignoring him; looking at a card.*]Who's the Reverend William Hackler? He wasn't the new assistant minister I met —

TOM: He's the Reverend of the Baptist Church on First Street.

FRANK: That was a black church.

TOM: It still is.

[*Short pause.*]

LIBBY: Mom did a lot of volunteer work there these past couple of years. I just found out about it myself.

TOM: A few weeks ago Hackler shows up at the hospital — And he and Mom begin to have this conversation . . . [*Beat.*] She told no one what she was doing.

FRANK: [*Signs his name and goes to another card.*] Mom. Dear Mom. [*He smiles and shakes his head.*]

TOM: What does that mean? [*Beat.*] What the hell does that mean?! [*Beat.*] You think it was stupid or something for her to volunteer to work at a black —

FRANK: Get off my back!!! [*Beat.*] I didn't say anything. [*Beat.*] Mom was a character, okay? We all knew that. One lovable, a bit eccentric, maybe overly generous character.

[*Short pause. To* LIBBY.] He wants to turn me into a racist now. [*Laughs.*] Why?? Because I happen to disagree with him on a few things. Tolerant, aren't we. Tom? [*Beat.*] What else are you going to beat your chest about? Next will it be that I'm anti-semitic because I don't happen to pray every morning in the direction of your *New York Times*?!! [*Laughs.*] You should really see the rest of this country, Tom. You should see just what a dinosaur you have become.

[*To* LIBBY.] I have a Chicano nurse and secretary, Libby. The son of one I'm helping through college. The University of Arizona.

[*To* TOM.] I try to help where I can. What the hell do you do, besides lecture people?!! [*Beat.*] You want to know who is really closer to Mom, to the kind of help she was trying to —

TOM: [*Yells.*] You aren't!! You aren't!!

[FRANK *is laughing.*]

LIBBY: Stop laughing Frank.

[*Pause. They continue to sign cards.*]

TOM: [*To* LIBBY.] Tell me, am I crazy or what, but wasn't there a time long ago when the word "conservative" meant something — *bad?*

[*Beat. Then* LIBBY *laughs and* TOM *laughs.*]

FRANK: I don't know, was it ever bad to *eat* conservatively, *drive* conservatively, *drink* conservatively, which, after watching you these past two days, Tom, I suggest you begin to think about.

[*Short pause.*]

TOM: [*To* LIBBY.] First they appropriate the flag, now they're after "health." Incredible.

FRANK: The flag we didn't wait to appropriate, we grabbed it out of your hands to stop you from burning it.

TOM: The hypocrisy! [*Beat.*] Or is it amnesia? [*To* LIBBY.] You remember, don't you, sitting up with Mom and Dad and Frank and listening to them make plans for Frank to go to Canada?

FRANK: I didn't go, did I?

TOM: Because of the lottery. You got something like three hundred and thirty in the lottery!!

FRANK: You want to know what I think you people's problem is?

TOM: Who's "you people"?

FRANK: [*Ignoring him.*] You have to make everything a world cause. Everyone has to join in. Everyone has to follow you. Think like you. Believe in what you believe. But things have changed, Tom. Look around. Take a trip. Come and visit us. [*Beat.*] What you'll realize, I swear to you, is that you need to relax. I say this as a brother. Look at your drinking for Christ sake.

TOM: I don't drink —

FRANK: Mom was relaxed. You want to be like her? Keep her ideals alive? Okay. But she didn't try and change the world. She didn't make a big *show* out of what she did. You just said that yourself. [*Beat.*] Why does one person feel the need to impose his beliefs on another person? This is what I do not get. People are not as dumb as you people in the East think they are. [*Beat.*] Politics. Politics. Where does that get you? Lay off for a while; I promise you, it'll change your life. [*Beat.*] Always attacking everything. Standing up for what? Attack attack blame blame. Like with Mom's death. She died for Christ sake, let her lie in peace. Let us live in peace. [*Beat.*] Just get on with life. Move on.

TOM: Grow up?

FRANK: Your words, not mine, but I'm not arguing. [*Short pause.*] So — yeh, grow and begin for a change to look at things positively. You'll be amazed what a relief it is to stop finding fault with everything. I promise, you'll feel good.

JUDITH: [*Entering with coffee.*] Sorry I took so long with the coffee, but —

TOM: [*To* FRANK, *interrupting.*] Is that the point now, Frank — to feel good?

FRANK: What is wrong with that? [*Beat.*] I see nothing wrong with that.

[*Short pause.*]

JUDITH: Uh, I did a little cleaning around the stove, that's why — If the real estate people are coming by —

LIBBY: What real estate people — ?

FRANK: Just to set a price. Just so we can see what it's worth. I figured while we're still here — I know we haven't decided to sell. I'm not pushing anything. I'm just getting the facts.

[JUDITH *sets down the coffee.*]

I'll get those colored stickers. They're in Tom's car.

TOM: It's open.

FRANK: [*Starts to leave, stops.*] I'm glad we talked, Tom. [*Beat.*] It seems like years, doesn't it? Don't misunderstand me, I know there are a lot of things wrong with the world, but — and this is a big "but" — things are also not as bad as you think.

TOM: Maybe not for you.

[*Pause.*]

FRANK: So, I am one of the fortunate ones. You think I should be sorry for that?

[*He goes. Short pause.*]

JUDITH: No one takes sugar, do they?

LIBBY: I do.

JUDITH: Oh. [*Beat.*] I'll check in the pantry.

LIBBY: [*Without meaning it.*] I can look if you —

JUDITH: No, no. Let me. It's been a hard day for all of you, I'm sure.

[*She goes. Pause.*]

TOM: [*Finally.*] Listen.

LIBBY: What?

TOM: Hear that?

LIBBY: What? No.

TOM: It's Mom and Dad. [*Beat.*] They must have been listening. [*Beat.*] Because they're crying now.

[*BLACKOUT.*]

Aaron Sorkin

HIDDEN IN THIS PICTURE
A Play in One Act

HIDDEN IN THIS PICTURE

REPRINTED BY PERMISSION OF: The Author.

COPYRIGHT: 1989

Aaron Sorkin

Aaron Sorkin received the Outer Critic Circle Award for his play *A Few Good Men*. He is the author of an expanded version of *Hidden In This Picture* titled *Making Movies*, which played off-Broadway at the Promenade Theatre. A 1983 graduate of the Syracuse University drama department, Mr. Sorkin has contributed to *Rolling Stone*, *New York Newsday* and *Playbill Magazine*.

A small, grassy hill overlooking a massive expanse of land. On this plateau sits a directors chair. Next to the directors chair sits a bottle of champagne and two glasses.

AT RISE: ROBERT *is standing and surveying the scene before him. He is in his early thirties. He wears jeans, boots, a baseball cap, a windbreaker, and sunglasses. Around his neck on a piece of string is a camera lens. Although he shows all the signs of a man who has not had enough sleep, he is, at the moment, as content as he's ever been. He checks his pocket watch. After a moment,* REUBEN *enters. He is in his early forties and is inappropriately dressed in a jacket and tie. Mud has begun to cake to his shoes and the bottom of his slacks. He's out of breath.*

REUBEN: Uh . . . Robert . . . What are you doing?

ROBERT: [*Not paying much attention.*] Hm?

REUBEN: [*Shouting Off-Right and down.*] He's up here!

ROBERT: This is perfect, did you know that?

REUBEN: [*Shouting.*] Sylvia! He's up here!

ROBERT: This is a perfect shot.

REUBEN: Robert —

ROBERT: This is an Academy Award winning shot.

REUBEN: Robert, what are you doing up here?

ROBERT: Looking at my Academy Award winning shot.

REUBEN: They give Academy Awards for *movies*, Robert, not shots. And if they gave Academy Awards for shots, it's a pretty good bet that the shot would actually have to be down on *film*. It's not like we can invite the members of the Academy out here to the location and say "Look at this shot", am I making sense? Robert, we have four minutes to sunset.

ROBERT: Four minutes and ten seconds.

REUBEN: Oh, good, sorry, I didn't know. Let's go square dancing.

ROBERT: Don't bug me, Reuben. I'm happy right now. I'm trying to make believe you're not here right now.

REUBEN: Robert — Bobby — Lindstrom and Sachs were serious. They were dead serious, I know what I'm talking about. There's no more money. There is no more money. There was no more money two weeks ago when you were three weeks behind and six and a half million over. There was no money *then*. There is now *officially* no more money. I don't like being an asshole, but it's my job. I'm the Production Manager. I'm here to see that things run on schedule and at budget.

ROBERT: Three weeks behind and six and a half million over?

REUBEN: That's right.

ROBERT: You've been doing a good job, Reuben.

REUBEN: The final shot, Robert, *one shot*, and then the crew, the cast, the six-hundred and ninety-four extras, the cameras, the lights, the food, the trailers, they all go home.

ROBERT: We're gonna go home Reuben, it's under control, trust me.

REUBEN: You've said that before.

ROBERT: I was lying.

REUBEN: There's no re-take, here, you understand that, don't you? We can't ask the sun to come back and set again because we screwed it up the first time.

ROBERT: We can't?

REUBEN: No.

ROBERT: What if we asked nicely?

REUBEN: Goddamit —

ROBERT: What if we call the sun's agent?

REUBEN: I'm not fuckin' around.

ROBERT: Neither am I. Call William Morris, find out who handles the sun, say we need a little favor. Say there's the possibility that we might have to re-take a shot and, in the event that we do, is there any chance the sun would be willing to come back up and set again. I mean, you know, we'll owe him one.

REUBEN: Three and a half minutes, Robert. Don't you think you should be down with the crew?

ROBERT: The crew knows what to do.

REUBEN: How the hell do you know?

ROBERT: [*For the first time, he stops gazing out in the distance. He takes his sunglasses off and speaks directly to* REUBEN.] Because we've been rehearsing for the past six hours. Because despite the fact that this is my first film, a fact that you've seen fit to remind me of four times a day since pre-production, despite that fact, I'm not an idiot. Because, whether you know it or not, and I suspect you don't, this is the most important shot in the movie and I have no intention of screwing it up. Because I have left absolutely no room for human error, Reuben. At seven thirty-seven the sun will begin to set. A seven thirty-seven the cameras will roll, three of them. Two Pana-flex 8-80's and an Aeri-BL. There is film in the cameras and the focus is pulled, I've checked them all six times. There are security guards posted by the cameras at the foot of the hill and there are twenty-six kids out of UCLA with walkie-talkies posted around the perimeter of the shot. Eleven minutes and thirty seconds. The cameras will roll for eleven minutes and thirty seconds. And during that eleven minutes and thirty seconds, our six-hundred and ninety-four extras, already costumed and approved in their uniforms, will, in a slow, trickling, symphonically theatrical stream, trot the four-thousand, five-hundred and sixty foot diagonal from the ridge of those trees, down past the blue flag and out of camera range. Roll credits. Six hours we rehearsed, Reuben, you should've been here. I ran them, and I ran them, and I ran them. And they got it right the first time. Craig is down on the deck, he'll be calling it. And when he does, there isn't a man, woman, or child who doesn't know what they're supposed to do. So I staked out this hill, and Jeff's gonna join me, and together we're going to watch art being made.

REUBEN: They're serious, Robert, this is it. Whatever you've got goes in the can and if it's not releaseable, they'll eat it, I swear, they can afford it.

ROBERT: I thought you said there was no more money?

REUBEN: Not for this. Not for a movie about disillusioned Marines in Guam playing war games that everyone in the industry knows is not going to make doo-dah at the box office!

ROBERT: [*Pause.*] If they didn't *like* the movie, why'd they *make* the movie?

REUBEN: The hell did they know, they liked your plays.

ROBERT: They weren't my plays, they were Jeff's plays.

REUBEN: Your plays, Jeff's plays, who gives a shit?

ROBERT: Jeff, probably. Jeff's mom.

REUBEN: They went to New York, they went to the theatre, they saw a play. You directed, Jeff wrote it, they said "You guys wanna make a movie? Here's some money." They gave you money, a crew, equipment, actors —

ROBERT: Actors —

REUBEN: You have a problem with the actors?

ROBERT: No, sir.

REUBEN: These actors were pussycats, Robert, lemme tell you, these actors were dolls.

ROBERT: The actors never liked me, Reuben.

REUBEN: The actors loved you. You couldn't remember their names. *You* didn't like the *actors*.

ROBERT: That's right, I forgot.

REUBEN: And I'm asking you, did you have a problem with these actors? Did you have one attitude case? One star trip? One prima donna? Can you tell me that they were really a problem?

ROBERT: No, they were not a problem. Talentless and vacuous, sure. Vapid, facile, a little insipid . . . Good, looking, though. Some of the best looking actors I've ever seen, I swear. But no, they weren't hard to get along with.

REUBEN: I'm sorry, my friend, but there was a limit to what could be done with the material.

ROBERT: Jeff worked very hard on this screenplay.

REUBEN: Yeah? Well it's lousy. It's full of Yale Drama crap. He should've stayed in church basements in SoHo where if the audience doesn't understand what the fuck is going on, they give him a plaque. I got news for you, welcome to the movies, if the audience doesn't understand what the fuck is going on, they leave. And they tell their friends. And they don't rent the video cassette. An we lose the European market. And there's no sequel. And there's no ancillary sales. And if you think I'm some kind of mercantile, anti-artist, studio-puppet, who only sees dollars and cents, you're right. But that's my job. And all I have to say is that if you expect to be handed seventeen-million dollars to make a movie, with another ten-million to promote it, you better be pretty damn sure that someone in Des Moines is gonna buy a ticket. You have two minutes and twenty-seconds.

[JEFF *enters. He's around the same age as* ROBERT *and wears jeans, sneakers, and a fatigue jacket.*]

JEFF: Reuben! Great! I have a question for you. Those people down there with the walkie-talkies . . . they work for us?

REUBEN: Yes.

JEFF: Good. I've fallen in love with one of them. I don't know her name, but she's got red hair and she's wearing blue pants and a white sweatshirt. If you could casually mention some impressive things about me to her, I would genuinely appreciate it. [REUBEN stares at him. JEFF *takes out a note pad and pen.*] I'll jot some down

ROBERT: Reuben's in a bad mood, Jeff.

JEFF: Why?

ROBERT: He thinks I've spent too much time and too much money making a movie about disillusioned Marines in Guam and he thinks your screenplay is full of Yale Drama crap and he thinks that no one in Des Moines is gonna buy a ticket.

JEFF: I'm not sure I'd say the Marines are disillusioned.

REUBEN: I'm going back down to the deck. You have two minutes.

JEFF: [*Calling after him.*] Reuben! [JEFF *scribbles something on a note and hands it to him.*] This is important to me. Red hair, blue pants, white sweatshirt. Tell her I have a reputation. [*To* ROBERT, *who has gone back to staring off in the distance.*] Champagne?

ROBERT: Oh yeah.

[CRAIG *enters. He's about the same age as* ROBERT *and* JEFF. *He wears glasses and carries a walkie-talkie in his belt.*]

CRAIG: Bob, we're at stand-by.

ROBERT: How's it look?

CRAIG: No problems.

ROBERT: It's your call.

CRAIG: I wanted to thank you for this.

ROBERT: Thank me for what?

CRAIG: Well, for giving me control like this. For letting me call a shot. It really means a lot to me.

ROBERT: You've done a real good job, I mean that. Nothing to thank me for.

CRAIG: It's just that I was a production assistant for four years, and all I've ever really gotten to do was organize background.

ROBERT: I'm sure you can handle it, Craig.

CRAIG: And I wanted to express my appreciation for your confidence in me, Bob.

ROBERT: Don't mention it.

CRAIG: It's just that I wanted you to know that you're the first person who's ever really considered that I might have, you know, some sort of personal career goals beyond being an A.D.

ROBERT: Craig, I hate to seem cold right now, 'cause I can tell you're opening up a little to me and I think that's great, but you are planning on going back down to the deck and call the shot aren't you?

CRAIG: Sure. [*He doesn't move.*]

ROBERT: I mean you understand that the cameras are not gonna roll unless you call action, you understand that, don't you?

CRAIG: I'm not stupid, Bob.

ROBERT: [*Pause.*] No, of course not. I just wasn't sure whether or not you realized that we were inside two minutes.

CRAIG: [*Checks his watch.*] Yeah, one thirty-five.

ROBERT: I need help, Jeff.

JEFF: Craig, Bobby wants you to go down to the deck right now. He wants you to go down there because you have an extremely important job to do and he wants to be sure that you do it as well as he knows you're able.

CRAIG: Well that's what I was just saying to Bob. That I'm grateful to be given this responsibility and that I genuinely appreciate Bob's confidence in my ability to —

ROBERT: *GET DOWN ON THE DECK! RIGHT NOW! OR I WILL GO DOWN AND CALL THE SHOT MYSELF AND YOU WILL DIRECT TRAFFIC THE REST OF YOUR LIFE.*

CRAIG: Thank you, Bob. I mean it. [*He exits.*]

ROBERT: He's sweet.

JEFF: Yeah, and very quick.

ROBERT: Yeah.

JEFF: Why're you letting him call the shot?

ROBERT: Craig can call the play by play of the Yankees game for all the difference it'll make, the cameras have been rolling for the last ten minutes.

JEFF: You're kidding me.

ROBERT: In a minute forty-five, Hillary will radio Michael who's standing by at the ridge, and Michael will cue the Marines.

JEFF: You've been letting the cameras roll for ten minutes?

ROBERT: Craig 'll never know. What's the harm? He can go home and tell people he called the final shot of the film, and they will have sex with him.

JEFF: Bobby, three cameras rolling for ten minutes, and now they're gonna roll for another eleven and a half? At a thousand dollars a foot per camera?

ROBERT: You sound like Reuben, Jeff, it's not your money.

JEFF: It's *somebody's* money and it's being spent irresponsibly.

ROBERT: I want this shot.

JEFF: You'll get this shot.

ROBERT: I'm making sure.

JEFF: You're becoming obsessive.

ROBERT: If not now, when, Jeff? In the editing room? You know how many people get to cut this movie before I do? About the same number who get to cut it *after* I do. The unit caterer has more artistic control over this project than I've been given. Well fuck it, Jeff, I'm getting this shot. I've created a picture here, I've communicated with an image. I've communicated an idea, an emotion, *my* idea, and I've done it as succinctly as a well written sentence and as powerfully as a symphony. The rest of this film may end up looking like Beaver Goes to War, but this shot, this image, is gonna work.

JEFF: Good luck.

ROBERT: [*Checking his watch.*] Forty-five seconds.

JEFF: [*Pause.*] Who's Hillary?

ROBERT: Red hair, blue pants, white sweatshirt.

JEFF: Hillary.

ROBERT: [*Pause.*] Thirty-five seconds. Thirty-five seconds till my dream comes true. How many times can you say that, Jeff?

JEFF: You mean, how many times can I say it really fast? I've never been good at that.

ROBERT: Please, God. Please be perfect, God. Just nice and slow and easy, God. No mistakes. I'm not asking any special favors of you, God, I'm not asking you to interfere. I've got all the bases covered, God, now please just let me have this. God, for the next eleven and a half minutes, just make the sun go down behind that hill and then mind your own business.

JEFF: Bobby —

ROBERT: Ssh. [*Pause. Whispering.*] Action. [*Pause.*] Oh yeah. Oh. Oh my. This is for my children, Jeff. This is for my little daughter. This is for Jennifer who'll watch it with her friends and say "My Daddy did that." This is for my unborn son who'll look at this and say "I want to be just like my Dad." This isn't for the actors, Jeff, this isn't for Lindstrom and Sachs, this isn't even for you. This one's for me. Look at it, Jeff, look at it.

JEFF: I'm looking.

ROBERT: Yeah, but are you seeing it?

JEFF: I think so. I'm looking at it.

ROBERT: Try and see it. Put a frame around it and see the picture.

JEFF: [*Pause.*] Yeah.

ROBERT: Are you looking at it?

JEFF: I'm seeing it, Bobby.

ROBERT: Communicating an idea. Causing emotion. No words. No sounds. No paints. No brushes. Just twelve-hundred acres in Central New York, Six-hundred and ninety-four extras jogging down a hill, three, four, six at a time, and a perfect sunset. I don't know that I've ever been more fulfilled than I am right now.

JEFF: [*Pause.*] You don't happen to know if Hillary's married or anything, do you?

ROBERT: Jeff.

JEFF: Sorry.

ROBERT: Jesus.

JEFF: I was looking, I was looking.

ROBERT: You know, when you've written a scene, and you're excited about it, I like to think that I'm pretty supportive. I like to think, you know, when you've created something that pleases you, that I share your enthusiasm whether it's genuine or not.

JEFF: Whether it's genuine or not?

ROBERT: Yes, Jeff. I'm not always as bowled over by your dramaturgy as I, perhaps, have sometimes led you to believe, on occasion. But that's not the point. The point is that I'm your friend, and I'm an artist, and I know how important it is to have an inspiration or whatever, you know — what?

JEFF: Nurtured?

ROBERT: Yeah.

JEFF: Whether it's genuine or not?

ROBERT: Yes. I encourage you. I support you. I celebrate with you.

JEFF: Except that in addition to being my friend and being an artist, you've also directed the last three plays that I've written. You've been the director, Bobby. And as the director, I depend upon your skilled, trained, experienced, and objective eye to guide me through a very crucial polishing a focusing process prior to and during the rehearsal period. I appreciate the gesture, but in the future I'd like it, and I'll think you'll find in the long run that it will be more valuable and rewarding, if you told me exactly what you thought of my work.

ROBERT: I think your work has a tendency to be long winded and cynical, I think you have difficulty handling exposition, I think you take forever to introduce the inciting action, and I think your female characters talk and behave as if they just stepped off of the Love Boat.

JEFF: I said "In the future," Bobby. In the *future* I'd like you to be honest, and *specific*, about problems you might have with my work, so that I may reasonably ascertain whether I should heed your suggestions or seek another director. In the future, Bob. Not while I'm watching, sorry, seeing this communication of emotion. [*Beat.*] And let me just say that while I give you full credit for creating this, the final scene of the picture, without sounds, without paints, without brushes, but for the 127 pages of dialog which precedes your creation, this would be a scene about a bunch of guys running down a hill. For eleven and a half minutes.

[CRAIG *enters.*]

CRAIG: So far, so good.

ROBERT: Doin' a great job, Craig. Everything looks perfect.

CRAIG: Everything's goin' smooth as can be, Bob.

ROBERT: Love to hear it. How's the timing?

CRAIG: The starting pace was about ten seconds fast, I called up to Michael and we straightened it out.

ROBERT: What'd you tell him?

CRAIG: I told him to have the Marines slow down a little.

ROBERT: Good call, Craig, you did the right thing.

CRAIG: Thank you, I appreciate that.

ROBERT: Well . . . I'm glad I have you down there. [*Beat.*] Down on the deck.

CRAIG: No, I mean it. I know you've got a lot on your mind right now and that, I mean, you could use some, you know, you're really tired, but I just think it's nice that you took the time and had the inclination to, you know . . . say that.

ROBERT: Craig, I need you on the deck.

CRAIG: I just came up to tell you that everything was going fine.

ROBERT: And I appreciate that. But I can see that everything is fine from right here. I can see everything from here. That's why I'm here. If all three cameras burst into flames at once, I'll know the moment that you know.

JEFF: Maybe even sooner.

ROBERT: The thing that I can't do from up here, is get timings from Hillary and relay instructions to Michael.

CRAIG: You want me to rig you up with a walkie-talkie?

ROBERT: I want you to — [*Resigning and asking for help.*] — Jeff.

JEFF: I don't know, Bobby, why don't you try communicating an emotion to Craig with an image. You don't need words. Long winded, cynical, clumsily expository, tensionless, sexist, soap operatic words.

CRAIG: Bob, I'm gonna get back down to the deck. I'll check the timings.

ROBERT: Thank you. [CRAIG *exits*.] Jeff, I apologize. I didn't mean to hurt your feelings. I don't — I just made that all up, I'm sorry, it was nasty and inappropriate. Jeff, we're coming up to the real meat of the sunset and I'd just like to watch it. [*Throughout this,* JEFF *has been staring at a spot off in the distance and to the right.*]Jeff, just let me live this next ten minutes with your blessing and your forgiveness and then we can fight if you want. I'll do whatever you want,I'll tell Hillary you've got a three picture deal at Warners. Please, shake hands with me and watch my scene.

JEFF: Bobby?

ROBERT: Jeff?

JEFF: [*Pause.*] Three cows have walked into the shot.

ROBERT: [*Long pause. He must have heard wrong.*] I'm sorry, what did you say?

JEFF: Three cows have walked into the shot.

[ROBERT *turns and looks out.*]

ROBERT: There are cows in the shot.

JEFF: Three.

ROBERT: Three cows are in the shot.

JEFF: Yeah.

ROBERT: I don't understand.

JEFF: Three cows are grazing in the middle of the shot.

ROBERT: Jesus Christ Almighty. [*He runs off. We hear him yelling, getting fainter and fainter in the distance.*] YOU'RE IN THE SHOT! GET OUT OF THE SHOT! COWS! GET THE HELL OUT OF THE SHOT!

[*Long pause.* ROBERT *returns.*]

ROBERT: Before I even beging to try and solve this problem, I want you to tell me, Jeff, you wrote the screenplay, you did research, you did months of research, you read books, tell me, are there cows on Guam?

JEFF: Not on Marine bases.

ROBERT: Fuck. [*Beat.*] Fuck, fuck, fuck. [*Beat.*] Never?

JEFF: No, never. There are no cows on Marine bases. Anywhere. Guam, Nicaragua, Berlin, there are no cows.

ROBERT: Don't tell me there are no cows, there are three cows standing in the middle of the shot!

JEFF: That's because we're ten miles outside of Schenectady on a farm. We're only pretending we're on a Marine base. The cows aren't screwin' around, they're on a farm. Bobby, it's okay. Just have some guys run out there and kinda shoo away the cows.

ROBERT: Shoo away the cows?

JEFF: Yeah, get a couple a guys to run out there and sorta herd 'em off to the left.

ROBERT: Jeff, an entire Marine infantry unit is running toward them with machine guns. They're not moving anywhere.

JEFF: It's 'cause they're all running past them. The cows probably can't even see them. Send some people out to run right towards them and herd 'em off that way to the left. You can edit this stuff out and the scene'll be nine minutes instead of eleven minutes. [*Pause.*] Bobby, it's the only thing to do.

ROBERT: Those cows have gotta be three-quarters of a mile away. We've got eight minutes left. Do you know how long it's gonna take to get a film crew to run three-quarters of a mile up hill, clear the cows from the shot and then clear themselves from the shot? *What the fuck are they doing there?*

JEFF: It looks like they're eating.

ROBERT: Oh, good. And on this twelve-hundred acre farm in the middle of *nowhere*, it was important that these cows eat *that* particular spot of grass. And I'm sure that it was *very* important that they eat right *now*. I'm sure that they have many appointments later in the evening, leaving them no choice but to grab a quick bite during *this* particular eleven minute period.

[CRAIG *enters.*]

CRAIG: Bobby, three cows have walked into the shot. I think it's pretty noticeable.

ROBERT: Oh? What makes you say that, Craig, what makes you say it's noticeable?

CRAIG: Well ... everybody noticed.

ROBERT: Jeff —

JEFF: Listen to me, just sit tight.

ROBERT: The sun is setting, Jeff. Seemingly faster than it's ever set before.

JEFF: You might be able to salvage enough ending footage and then fudge around with the continuity on the sunset.

ROBERT: If the cows move. If they decide to move back out of the shot.

JEFF: Right.

ROBERT: And if they don't?

JEFF: You're screwed.

ROBERT: What's goin' on, God? Why are you doing this to me? Please move the cows, God. Move 'em over seventy-five yards to the left, God, what's the big deal? I'm not kidding, I'm really at a complete — I don't know what I'm supposed to do? Are you — Wait, wait, wait, what are they doing? They're bobbing their heads or something. What does that mean? Do you think that means they're ready to leave? Does it seem to you that they're about ready to leave?

JEFF: I don't — I'm not a livestock psychologist, Rob, I don't know if the cows seem ready to leave.

CRAIG: I think they're about ready to leave.

JEFF: Craig, on the other hand, has a very strong sense that the cows will be leaving soon.

ROBERT: Would you look at those guys? Just trotting by these cows like they weren't there. Doing it exactly the way we did it in rehearsal. You'd sorta think that one of 'em would say to himself "Hm, I'm an actor and I'm supposed to be imitating life. Right now I'm playing a Marine on my way back to the barracks. There's a cow. If I were a Marine, I'd probably think it was somewhat out of the ordinary to see a cow on my way back to my barracks. I should use what's around me. I should use what's really happening, both externally and internally." You'd think one of those guys would somehow acknowledge the fact that they're running past three cows on the way down the hill.

CRAIG: Should I call Michael?

ROBERT: Please.

CRAIG: What should I tell him?

ROBERT: Tell him to tell whoever is left up there, that the scene now includes three cows. Tell him to tell whoever is left, that there's no point ignoring the cows, it only makes us look stupid.

CRAIG: I left my walkie-talkie down on the deck.

ROBERT: Go. [CRAIG *begins to leave.*] Hold it. Don't bother. The extras have discovered the cows. They're acting with the cows. The extras are doing bits of business with the cows. I hate those cows. [*Beat.*] You know what I think? I think that it's not nearly as big a problem as we think it is.

JEFF: Truly, Robert, that's the attitude you gotta have.

ROBERT: 'Cause you know why? 'Cause I don't think anyone in the audience is gonna notice. I mean, sure, they're gonna notice, they're gonna see these three cows in silhouette against a sunset while 694 Marines file back to their barracks after having spent the most difficult day of their lives engaged in a war game, sure the audience is gonna see these cows, *but I don't think they're gonna find that strange.*

JEFF: You don't?

ROBERT: No.

JEFF: Why not?

ROBERT: Why should they? They're just cows. Everybody's seen cows. What's the big scream? They're cows.

JEFF: On a Marine compound? In Guam?

ROBERT: You think people are gonna pick that out?

JEFF: I hope so. I mean if they've just sat through a two hour movie and they don't know that it took place on a Marine compound in Guam, hell, I think we can put Rocky and Bullwinkle out there and it won't make a difference.

ROBERT: I don't know, call it instinct, I don't think people are gonna find that strange.

JEFF: I find it a little strange. You find it strange.

CRAIG: I find it strange.

JEFF: Craig finds it strange, you wanna talk about playing to the lowest common denominator.

ROBERT: [*To* CRAIG.] You find it strange?

CRAIG: Pretty strange, yeah.

ROBERT: [*Makes up his mind.*] I want you to call down to the deck. Talk to Hillary. Get one of the policemen, one of the Schenectady Police guys, are they still around?

CRAIG: Yeah.

ROBERT: Good. I want you to radio down to the deck. Tell Hillary to have the policemen shoot the cows.

JEFF: Bobby —

ROBERT: Call!

JEFF: Craig, stop. Bobby, you can't tell the police to shoot the cows.

ROBERT: Why not?

JEFF: Why not? For about ten different reasons.

ROBERT: I don't have time for ten, gimme one.

JEFF: You can't kill cows to make a movie.

ROBERT: We kill cows to make hamburgers, why can't I kill cows to make a movie, what's the difference?

JEFF: What's the difference between food and a movie? Are you serious?

ROBERT: They don't have to kill the cows, they don't have to shoot to kill, just drop 'em . Wound 'em for crying out loud, I'm running out of time.

JEFF: Bobby, allow me a very quick hypothetical. Let's assume for a moment that Schenectady police officers carry pistols that can fire three-quarters of a mile and that the officers are accurate at that range so as to be able to wound and not kill a cow. Fast forward a year. Don't you think, now come on, don't you think that even the people who *don't* find it a little strange that three cows have wandered into Guam are gonna be a little perplexed when the cows, for no apparent reason, fall down to the ground?

ROBERT: You're right.

JEFF: I know.

ROBERT: You're one-hundred percent right.

JEFF: So just relax. The cows'll leave, you'll salvage some footage. The scene was too long anyway.

ROBERT: I've been looking at this all wrong. Look at the cows. What do they look like to you?

JEFF: The cows?

ROBERT: Yeah.

JEFF: They look like cows.

ROBERT: Besides cows. What do they look like besides cows?

JEFF: I'm not sure I understand.

ROBERT: I'm saying look at the cows, and tell me what you think they look like other than cows.

JEFF: I'm sorry, Rob, I'm drawing a blank. I'm looking at the cows and the only thing leaping out at me is that they look like cows.

ROBERT: Don't you think they look a little like tanks?

JEFF: Tanks?

ROBERT: Tanks. Sherman tanks. Don't you think they look a little, in a way, off in the distance there in silhouette, like tanks?

JEFF: No.

ROBERT: What do you think they look like?

JEFF: I think they look like cows.

ROBERT: Forget about the cows. Cows aren't an option, you can't choose cows, they're not cows.

JEFF: But they are cows. And they look like cows. Which only makes sense, 'cause they are cows.

ROBERT: I'm asking you to use your imagination, Jeff. I'm asking you to, for once in your life, be emotional and not intellectual. I'm asking you to pretend, to reach back in your mind's eye and tell me what you see, other than cows, when you look at those cows.

JEFF: You want me to be emotional and not intellectual?

ROBERT: Please. Once. For me.

JEFF: I see love, Rob. I see children playing freeze-tag in a sunny meadow. I see Fifth Avenue at Christmas time. I see a rainy Sunday afternoon by the fireplace. I see a man at peace with himself.

CRAIG: Really? Kids playing freeze-tag?

JEFF: *I see cows, Bobby!*

ROBERT: You don't think they look like Sherman tanks?

JEFF: Rob, you're out of control.

ROBERT: I'm in complete control. I know what I'm saying. I can make this work. If you — listen to me — if you squint your eyes a little and kinda blur things up, you see, I swear, they look like tanks. And no one's gonna think that's strange, right? I mean, tanks on a Marine base are okay. [*Beat.*] You don't think I'm right?

JEFF: No.

ROBERT: Why?

JEFF: Because I think that when the ushers in the theatre instruct the audience to squint their eyes a little bit, some of 'em, some of the audience, are gonna hold out. I think that some people in the audience will, just for curiosity's sake, not squint their eyes a little. I think it's even possible that some of the critics will not squint their eyes a little. And those people, the people who chose not to play along, will think the Sherman tanks look like cows. And they'll be right.

ROBERT: I'm not saying tell the audience to squint, Jeff. I'm not saying we have to have a guy go around the country shouting in dark movie theatres that the people should squint now.

JEFF: What are you saying?

ROBERT: We have footage of tanks. I mean, we already have the footage. We have feet and feet of footage of tanks. I just keep jump cutting for half a second at a time to these shots of tanks every couple of minutes, all the way through, just keep jump cutting to tanks, three, four frames a shot, they will be subliminally convinced that they're looking at tanks.

JEFF: Rob —

ROBERT: *They will be subliminally convinced!*

JEFF: Because you showed them tanks every once in a while they're gonna think those cows are tanks?

ROBERT: Yes!

JEFF: Who do you think your audience is?

ROBERT: Idiots, Jeff. I think the vast majority are lazy, stupid idiots who, I believe, can be convinced by a clever director with enough footage at his disposal that three cows are in fact Sherman tanks.

JEFF: Well you're wrong. The only person who thinks those cows are anything but cows is you.

ROBERT: Craig, what do the cows look like to you?

CRAIG: Those cows?

ROBERT: No, not those cows, Craig, other cows. Those cows.

CRAIG: I just didn't understand the question.

ROBERT: What do those cows look like to you? Those cows out there in the middle of the shot?

CRAIG: It's funny, I was just thinking, with the way they're sort of bobbing up and down while they eat —

ROBERT: Yeah, what Craig?

CRAIG: — and 'cause you can only really make them out in shadow,

ROBERT: Craig —

CRAIG: I was thinking that they looked a little like boats.

ROBERT: Boats.

CRAIG: Yeah. Boats tied to a mooring. Bobbing at their mooring.

JEFF: Do either of you have any sense of size? Do either of you have any sense of shape and proportion? Do either of you understand that a boat and a tank and a cow are three different things, or is it like, anything that can move is just sorta lumped into one big pile?

ROBERT: No, but we are film makers and we don't lock ourselves into conventional notions and labels. We give ourselves the freedom to explore and communicate our own surroundings and we don't file the world around us into little shoe-boxes and label them black and white.

JEFF: Those are cows, Bobby.

ROBERT: How do you know? Craig says they're boats.

CRAIG: I said they *looked* like boats.

JEFF: THEY LOOK LIKE COWS! They walk like cows! They eat like cows! They're cows! Accept that fact. I wouldn't lie to you about something like this. Boats float and tanks have guns and cows are standing right there. And they're noticeable. You can squint from now till Tuesday and they'll be cows. And I think they're the best thing in the movie.

ROBERT: [*Pause. Quietly.*] You're right. You're right. They're cows.

JEFF: What?

ROBERT: They're cows! There's really no way of getting around that. I thought there might be, but there isn't. They're cows. They'll have to stay cows. So fine. Okay. There are three cows standing in the last shot of the picture. [*Pause.*] What did I mean by that? What was I trying to say, I wonder? I need to examine this. What are cows? What *are* cows? Cows are cows. What do cows do? Cows give milk. Milk is life. Is milk life? No, not really. Milk is milk. But it's also life in a way. Sure. Milk. Mother's milk. The milk of life. [*Pause.*] Young, disillusioned Marines ... *Young* disillusioned Marines ... what? ... Sucking the milk of life ... the last drops of the milk of life, right? ... Sunset? Endings? The Last Drops? [*He's got it.*] Young disillusioned Marines sucking the last drops of life from cows ... Because their mother's aren't there with them in Guam! [*Beat.*] What am I saying?

CRAIG: Bob?

ROBERT: [*Quietly.*] Wrap it, Craig.

CRAIG: You sure?

ROBERT: Wrap it. I'll be down in a minute. I'd just like a minute before I go down there.

CRAIG: We still have about ninety seconds.

ROBERT: Don't waste film. Just cut it and let's go home.

CRAIG: Sure. [*He exits.*]

ROBERT: Go ahead. Say it.

JEFF: Say what?

ROBERT: Tell me how I never had control on this movie. Tell me about how I got ahead of myself. Tell me about how I got all dreamy and lofty and "master-filmmaker" and "boy-genius" and it all came crashing down around me and it's all capsulized, every one of my screw-ups, every one of my failed shots at the moon, they're all capsulized in this eleven minutes, which, I would say, will be coming soon to a theatre near you, except that I'm only a little luckier than that, Lindstrom and Sachs are gonna burn the negative. Go ahead. Say it, Jeff.

JEFF: I'm sorry, what am I supposed to say again?

ROBERT: Thank you, Jeff. Your compassion and sensitivity are moving me in a way I don't know what to do.

JEFF: Rob —

ROBERT: No go ahead. I'm serious, really. Have a little fun at my expense, Jeff.

JEFF: Rob, I wasn't gonna say that. I was gonna say let's go home, Rob. I was gonna say that the only reason why this movie sucks, and it really does bite, Rob, is that you had nothing to do with it. You were never in control and neither was I. They made us change things, we didn't even know why, we just did it. They's ask for a scene in bed, I'd write a scene in bed and it wasn't — Rob, it wouldn't even be *germane*. They surrounded you with — Did you hire *one* of these people yourself? You didn't make this movie, Rob, Lindstrom and Sachs did. They wrote it too. I *typed* it, that's what I did. Three months ago we were laughing about this, Bobby, you had a sense of humor about it. Come on, it's a bad movie, that's all. And it's not your fault. It's just a movie. A child hasn't died, Bobby.

ROBERT: I wish you wouldn't do that.

JEFF: Do what?

ROBERT: Talk about every problem in the world relative to the *worst* problem in the world. Just because one thing isn't as bad as something else, it doesn't make it good. It doesn't become all right. The town of Beaumont, Texas is flattened by a tornado, but "What's the problem? A nuclear weapon didn't explode." That's a bad habit, Jeff.

JEFF: Not when we're just talking about a movie.

ROBERT: That's not the point.

JEFF: What's the point?

ROBERT: The point is that Lindstrom and Sachs might just release the movie.

JEFF: So what?

ROBERT: *MY NAME'S ON IT!* What is the matter with you? In New York you spend half an hour wondering whether or not to change a comma. You don't sleep when we're doing a play. We have to put you in a hospital after the opening. Why don't you give a damn now?

JEFF: Because I take no pride whatsoever in this piece of work. Because this piece of work was mangled beyond my ability or interest in repairing it, by forces beyond my ability or interest to reason with. But they were paying me a lot of money, so what the hell?

ROBERT: Jeff, this isn't supposed to be a hobby. This isn't a weekend tennis match. This is supposed to be our lives. This is supposed to be what keeps us going, and you just sit there like, "Win some, you lose some.

JEFF: That's right. But it's *not* my life. And it's not yours. It's what we do for a living. And we're really good at it. And it's what we like working at more than anything else. Your life is Nancy, and Jennifer, and the Knicks, and the boat, and your dad, and the tomatoes . . . my life is Hillary, . . . I can't really think of anything else off the top of my head, but the point is that it's really just a movie.

ROBERT: I understand what you're saying.

JEFF: But?

ROBERT: Look, okay, you're right. This isn't the biggest tragedy in the world, but it's as least as bad, I mean, wouldn't you have to say that it's on a par with, like, my boat sinking? I mean, don't you think that if I called you and said "Jeff, I just went down to go sailing and I looked in the water and saw that overnight, my boat, on which I've spent many wonderful hours with my wife and daughter enjoying the pleasure of the outdoors and upon which I've spent many invaluable hours alone with the soothing company of the sea and into which I've put my heart, muscle and soul, has sunk beyond retrieval," you would express sympathy?

JEFF: Yes. If your boat sank, I'd say I was sorry.

ROBERT: And you don't think that this, although certainly not a tragedy on the scale of, say, the assassination of Abraham Lincoln, is at least as bad as my boat sinking?

JEFF: Does the boat have passengers?

ROBERT: No, just the boat. [*Pause.*] A forty-five thousand dollar boat that I haven't finished paying for yet that I named after my first dog.

JEFF: Yes. I think they are equally bad. I'm sorry your movie has cows in it.

ROBERT: Thank you.

JEFF: I *am* sorry.

ROBERT: Then help me.

JEFF: How?

ROBERT: Gimme some Yale Drama crap.

JEFF: What?

ROBERT: I need an explanation. I need an explanation for the cows.

JEFF: An explanation.

ROBERT: Yeah.

JEFF: Why?

ROBERT: Why?

JEFF: Yes.

ROBERT: Why do I need an explanation?

JEFF: Yeah.

ROBERT: Because I asked God for a favor and he wasn't listening. Now I'm asking you. I'm asking you for an explanation for the cows. Something good. Something real.

JEFF: Something real. Like actors playing trained Marines making sure their hair is in place before the cameras roll. Like war and death and killing being reduced to a series of wacky, zany scenes so that it'll be somehow palatable to the 16 to 21 audience. You know, Bobby, after a year of this, I think it takes a certain amount of arrogance to assume that when three cows walk half a mile into the last scene of the movie, God wasn't listening.

ROBERT: You don't believe in God.

JEFF: No, I don't. And I don't believe in movies. I believe in cows. There's some Yale Drama crap for you. [*Long pause.* JEFF *is looking out toward the cows. He smiles.*] Bobby, what's this scene about?

ROBERT: No, you're right. Let's go home.

JEFF: Listen to me. What's this scene about?

ROBERT: I give up.

JEFF: No, you're gonna like this. What's this scene about?

ROBERT: It's supposed to be about the end of the day, the end of the game.

JEFF: Yeah, but it's not anymore. What's it about now?

ROBERT: It's about three cows.

JEFF: No it's not. What's it about?

ROBERT: It's about the incongruity of —

JEFF: Nope.

ROBERT: It's about — wait — the difference, the contrast in —

JEFF: No, no, no.

ROBERT: Yes, how can you really, to a certain degree, juxtapose —

JEFF: Bobby —

ROBERT: Jeff, I'm saying, what we're seeing is —

JEFF; What was going on in the scene? Really. What was *actually* going on in the scene.?

ROBERT: [*Pause.*] Marines were running down a hill.

JEFF: Who?

ROBERT: Marines.

JEFF: Who were they *really*?

ROBERT: Really?

JEFF: Yes.

ROBERT: They were extras.

JEFF; They were *actors*. In . . . ?

ROBERT: A movie.

JEFF: When all of a sudden . . . ?

ROBERT: Three cows walked into the most important shot.

JEFF: Of ... ?

ROBERT: The movie.

JEFF: Which is about ... ?

ROBERT: Disillusioned Marines in Guam.

JEFF: A subject to which we did a ... ?

ROBERT: Disservice.

JEFF: What kind of disservice ... ?

ROBERT: A great disservice.

JEFF: Okay. Now. What's the scene about? Really? Not the Marines. Not the sunset. What was really happening?

ROBERT: A movie shot was being destroyed.

JEFF: And if you don't think that that's an appropriate ending for this picture, you don't know Yale Drama crap when it comes up and bites you in the ass.

ROBERT: [*Pause.*] It's a scene about a movie shot getting destroyed.

JEFF: I truly could not have written it better if I had a hundred years.

ROBERT: The scene is about a movie shot being ruined by three cows.

JEFF: Yes it is. And you are the boldest director since Welles.

ROBERT: A bad film, which began as a good film, about a group of Marines who join the Corps with an idealized, one might even say Hollywoodized, image of the Marines, but whose fantasies come crashing down around them, is ending with three cows walking into the last shot of the film itself.

JEFF: And you're telling me God doesn't hang around upstate New York?

[REUBEN *enters.*]

REUBEN: Robert, the buses are leaving. Robert?

ROBERT: I'm coming.

REUBEN: Those cows were a pain in the ass, huh? What the hell, we'll just matte 'em out when we cut it. Hell of a sight though. I swear, I almost pissed my pants.

ROBERT: Matte 'em out?

REUBEN: Yeah. Takes half a day.

ROBERT: Matte out the cows?

REUBEN: Yeah, you talk to Leonard next week.

ROBERT: Why would I want to matte out the cows?

REUBEN: What?

ROBERT: I rehearsed those cows, I auditioned over four-hundred cows. Those were my favorites, they were my first choice. You gotta admit, the camera loves 'em, Reuben.

REUBEN: You planned those cows?

ROBERT: You believe this guy? Reuben, don't you understand?

REUBEN: You mean —

ROBERT: The scene. The *scene*. It's the whole statement of the picture.

REUBEN: The cows.

ROBERT: Yeah.

REUBEN: Oh, you're talking about . . . Sure. I thought you were talking about something else. [*Pause.*] I liked it. [*Pause.*] I really did. [*Pause.*] The buses are heading back.

ROBERT: I'm right behind you.

REUBEN: [*Stops before leaving.*] I think it's gonna work.[REUBEN *exits.*]

JEFF: You ready to go?

ROBERT: [*Staring off in the distance.*] Hang on . . . now they're leaving. [*Calling off, as if to say "That's all!"*] THANK YOU! THAT'S A WRAP!

[*BLACKOUT.*]

Wendy Wasserstein

BOY MEETS GIRL

BOY MEETS GIRL

Wendy Wasserstein

Wendy Wasserstein is a resident playwright at New York's Playwrights Horizons Theatre off-Broadway. Her plays produced at Playwrights Horizons include *Any Women Can't*, *Montpelier PaZazz*, *Uncommon Women and Others*, (staged reading prior to Phoenix Theatre production) *Isn't Romantic*, *Miami*, a workshop of a musical with music and lyrics by Jack Feldman and Bruce Sussman, and *The Heidi Chronicles*. For PBS, *Uncommon Women and Others*, *The Sorrows of Gin* and *Drive She Said*. Screenplays: adaptaions of *The House of Husbands*, co-authored with Christopher Durang, and *The Object of My Affection* by Stephen McCauley. Ms. Wasserstein is a contributing editor of *New York Woman* magazine. She is author of *Bachelor Girl*, a collection of essays recently published by Knopf and *The Heidi Chronicles & Other Plays* published by Harcourt, Brace, Jovanovich. She is a recipient of NEA and Guggenheim grants and serves on the council of the Dramatics Guild. *The Heidi Chronicles* was written during a grant from the British-American Arts Association and the National Theatre Corporation of Washington, D.C. Ms. Wasserstein was awarded the 1989 Tony Award for Best Play, The Pulitzer Prize for Drama, The New York Drama Critics Circle Award, The Outer Critics Circle Award, The Drama Desk award, The Susan Smith Blackburn Prize and The Dramatists Guild's Hull-Warriner Award for *The Heidi Chronicles*.

CHARACTERS

Molly, thirty-three years old, single, successful, and quietly desperate. Every Saturday night, Molly sheds her doctorate in molecular microchips and slips into a Zandra Rhodes macromini. On the weekends, Molly is just another girl at The Trading Post, a popular café on the Columbus Avenue strip. Just another S.S.D.B.G. (Single /Successful/Desperate/Bachelor Girl) waiting for a discriminating Root Canal Man to invite her for an unfulfilling weekend at his summer share in the Hamptons. Molly, a native New Yorker, has recently begun considering relocating to the Sun Belt.

Dan, a successful creative director at B.B.D.&O. advertising agency. He is thirty-two, single, and having a ball. Every night, after twelve hours of Clio Award-winning work for his clients, Dan goes to the Odeon, where he eats poached salmon on grilled kiwi fruit at a table crowded with visual artists, conceptual artists, and performing artists. And every night, after picking up the tab, Dan swears that he, too, will one day give up his job and devote himself to art.

Dr. Susan, Molly's psychiatrist.

Stanley Tannenbaum, Ph.D., Dan's psychologist.

Her Majesty, The Queen, ruler of the Helmsley Palace.

Narrator

PROLOGUE

NARRATOR: On a spring morning in 1972, a senior at the Spence School was in Central Park, completing her science project on the reproductive cycle of flowering plants, when she saw an unmarked bus drop off twenty women in silk suits, bow ties, and sneakers on the corner of Eighty-ninth Street and Fifth Avenue. The girl took note; when she was in sixth grade, sneakers and suits had been cause for suspension.

Meanwhile, on the West Side, a middle-aged but very nice lady was on her way to Barney Greengrass, the Sturgeon King, on Eighty-ninth Street, when three cars — a Volvo, a BMW, and a Saab with M.D. plates and a "Save the Whales" bumper sticker — pulled up to Eighty-seventh Street and Amsterdam Avenue. Fifteen young men, whom the lady thought she recognized from her son's protest days at the University of Wisconsin, emerged from the cars. Before the gracious lady could offer them an Entenmann's cake, they jogged into a dilapidated brownstone and immediately began exposing brick and hanging spider plants.

And the city embraced these pioneers, who were dressed in 100-per-cent natural fabric. They prospered and they multiplied. From the now infamous drop-offs grew a new breed of New Yorkers, the Professionalites. Only their ratio of men to women, three to four, has remained constant.

What follows is a Love Story in One Act and Six Scenes between two of these sabra Professionalites: Dan and Molly.

SCENE ONE: *One night in late August,* DAN *has a yearning to talk to someone who knows Donna Karan but has moved on to Issey Miyake.* DAN *slips into the Trading Post, where the number of single women is a plague to the West Side zoning committee. It is here that he first sees* MOLLY, *seated at the bar. She is young, she is urban, she is professional. He knows immediately that* MOLLY *is the kind of new-fashioned girl he could bring home to his analyst's couch.* DAN *sits next to her.*

DAN: Hi.

MOLLY: Hi.

DAN: Do you come here often?

MOLLY: Never.

DAN: I don't either.

MOLLY: I'm waiting here for a friend. She selected this place. I think what's happening to the West Side is outrageous.

DAN: This is really an East Side singles kind of restaurant.

MOLLY: Yes, but it's here on the West Side, so we have to deal with it.

DAN: You sound like a concerned citizen.

MOLLY: Did you ever read any Kenneth Burke? In college, maybe? Lit. Crit.?

DAN: [*Immediately.*] Oh, sure.

MOLLY: He divides people into observers, spectators, and participants. I'm here strictly as a sociological observer. I love to watch people in New York. Otherwise I would never come to a place like this.

DAN: I wouldn't either. In my spare time I write film criticism.

MOLLY: [*More interested.*] Oh, you're a critic! Who do you write for?

DAN: I write for myself. I keep a film criticism journal.

MOLLY: I love film. Women in film particularly interest me. My favorites are Diane Kurys, Doris Dörrie, and Lee Grant.

DAN: I love women in film too.

MOLLY: [*Impressed.*] You're so direct and forthcoming. What do you do?

DAN: I'm a psychiatrist.

MOLLY: Individual, group, house calls?

DAN: Actually, I'm a creative director at the B.B.D.&O. advertising agency. But I think of it as psychology. Dealing with the individual's everyday dreams and desires. I'm in charge of the Scott Paper account.

MOLLY: Fascinating. I use tissues a lot. I've always wondered why.

DAN: What do *you* do?

MOLLY: I'm a systems analyst for American Express.

DAN: "Do you know me?"

MOLLY: [*Very straightforward.*] Not very well. But I'd like to.

DAN: [*Looks at her intently.*] Why don't we go somewhere a little less trendy to talk. I can tell these aren't your kind of people.

MOLLY: No, I don't belong here. This isn't my New York.

DAN: [*Helps her on with her coat.*] That's a nice jacket.

MOLLY: Donna Karan. But I've moved on to Issey Miyake.

DAN: [*Putting on a multilayered karate jacket.*] We have so much in common.

MOLLY: "It's a phenomenon." That's a quote from a song in *Gypsy*. "Small world, isn't it?" I love Stephen Sondheim.

DAN: I'm afraid I don't know much about theater. I'm a workaholic. You know, mid-thirties New York guy, longing for Real Relationship with Remarkable Woman, meanwhile finds fulfillment through his work.

MOLLY: I think I like you. But be careful, I have Fear of Intimacy.

DAN: The Bachelor Girl's Disease. I hear it's an epidemic.

MOLLY: I'm working with my shrink to get past it.

[*Pause as* DAN *looks at her.*]

DAN: I think I like you, too.

[*They begin to exit restaurant.*]

DAN: What about your girl friend?

MOLLY: Uh, ah, she told me if she wasn't here by now she wasn't coming.

DAN: Not a very reliable friend.

MOLLY: No, but she's working with her shrink to get past it.

[*They exit.*]

SCENE TWO: *Phil's Risotto, a risotto and cheese emporium.* DAN *and* MOLLY *stroll over to the counter arm in arm. It is mid-September.*

DAN: [*Ordering at the counter.*] We'll have lemon risotto, chanterelle risotto, spinach risotto salad, pesto tart, carrot ravioli, goat cheese, goat cheese with ash, and a half pound of American.

MOLLY: [*Surprised, almost disturbed.*] American?

DAN: Have you ever had real American cheese? Not the stuff they sell at the supermarket, but real American. [*He gives her a piece.*] Taste this.

MOLLY: [*Tasting.*] Oh, that's marvelous!

DAN: I've been rediscovering American food: peanut butter, grape jelly, Marshmallow Fluff, Scooter Pies, Chef Boyardee, bologna. It is unbelievable! If it's done correctly.

MOLLY: [*Softly.*] I love you.

DAN: Excuse me?

MOLLY: I love blue. I adore Kraft blue cheese dressing.

DAN: Well, if it's done correctly.

SCENE THREE: MOLLY *in the office of her psychiatrist,* DR. SUSAN. *It is October.*

MOLLY: [*Sneezes.*] Excuse me. I'm getting a cold.

DR. SUSAN: How do you feel about that?

MOLLY: Terrible. Tissues remind me of him. He says people should live together before they get married.

DR. SUSAN: How do you feel about that?

MOLLY: Sigourney Weaver and Glenn Close are married.

DR. SUSAN: How do you feel about that?

MOLLY: Living together was for kids in the late sixties and seventies. I'm a thirty-three-year-old woman.

DR. SUSAN: How do you fell about that?

MOLLY: I need a commitment. I want a family. I don't want to take a course at the New School on how to place a personal ad. Meryl Streep has three children already.

DR. SUSAN: Why do you always compare yourself to movie stars? You're not an actress.

MOLLY: That's true. That's really true! That's an incredible insight. Maybe my mother wanted me to be an actress. I hate her.

SCENE FOUR: DAN *in the office of his psychologist*, STANLEY TAN-NENBAUM, PH.D. *It is November.*

DAN: I don't think I want to make a commitment to Molly, but I'm afraid of what she'll say.

STANLEY TANNENBAUM, PH.D.: Well, let's put Molly in this chair, and then you can answer for her.

DAN: All right. [*Talking now to an empty chair.*] Molly, I don't think I want to make a commitment.

[DAN *gets up and sits in chair to answer as* MOLLY *would.*]

DAN: [*Pretending he's* MOLLY.] That's okay. I'm an observer. This is all a sociological investigation. Kenneth Burke divides people into spectators, partici —

[DAN *runs back to his seat to answer* MOLLY.]

DAN: [*Angry.*] Who the hell is Kenneth Burke? That is so pretentious, Molly!

DAN: [*As* MOLLY.] Not as pretentious as keeping a journal of film criticism.

DAN: [*Furious.*] You resent my writing! You want to swallow me up. If

I live with you, I won't be here anymore. I'll lose myself.

STANLEY TANNENBAUM, PH.D.: Did you hear what you just said?

DAN: I have it. Goddamn it! I have it. Fear of Intimacy. That Bachelor Girl's Disease. Why couldn't I just get burn-out?

SCENE FIVE: *Central Park West. The Thanksgiving Day Parade.* DAN *and* MOLLY *are watching floats of Bullwinkle and Superman pass by.*

MOLLY: [*Overcome by the sight of the floats.*] I love this parade. Gosh, I really love this parade. Reminds me of growing up here and of New York before there were Benetton shops and a Trump Organization.

DAN: I never imagined people actually grew up in New york.

MOLLY: It was different then. There were real neighborhoods. The ladies on Madison Avenue wore white gloves and ate mashed potatoes at the Kirby Allen Restaurant. Marjorie Morningstar and her family gathered for Sabbath dinners on Central Park West. All artists wore turtlenecks and played bongo drums in the Village. And every night at seven o'clock, men in top hats and tails tap-danced from Shubert Alley to the Winter Garden theater.

DAN: Really!

MOLLY: Well, I like to think so. Now everywhere I go all the women look like me.

DAN: What's so bad about that?

MOLLY: Nothing, it's just that it's all the same. I like the idea of a flower district, a theater district, a diamond district. The whole city is being renovated into Molly district. Dan, I have to confess. I hate goat cheese.

DAN: [*Softly.*] Me, too. But I love you.

MOLLY: Hmmmmmm?

DAN: I hate goat cheese, but I love blue. Molly, with Bullwinkle as my witness, I want to marry you. And every Thanksgiving we can bring our children here. And someday they'll tell someone they met at The Trading Post, "I love this parade, I grew up here."

MOLLY: [*No longer wistful.*] But will our children go to Trinity or the Ethical Culture School? They could probably learn Chinese at Trinity, but there are a lot of Wall Street parents. Ethical Culture is nice, but maybe it's too liberal, not enough attention to the classics. How 'bout Brearley? There's something to be said for an all-women's education. [*She kisses* DAN.] Dan, just think! We can raise a family of women filmmakers!!!!!

SCENE SIX: *The Helmsley Palace. The Grand Ballroom. An enormous wedding party.* DAN *and* MOLLY *are standing under the altar before* HER MAJESTY, THE QUEEN.

QUEEN: Dan, do you take this woman to be your wife? To love, be emotionally supportive of, have good dialogue with, as well as a country home in the Hamptons, Connecticut, or possibly upper New York State?

DAN: I do.

QUEEN: Molly, do you take this man to love, and at the same time maintain your career, spend quality time with the children, and keep yourself appealing by joining the New York Health and Racquet Club?

MOLLY: I do.

QUEEN: [*Addressing the wedding guests.*] I've known this coulpe for two hours. But I've stood guard at their honeymoon suite. Molly will be able to see her makeup in soft light in the bathroom mirror. Dan will be put at ease by the suit hangers that detach from the closet. And if Dan and Molly decide to get remarried someday, and return to the honeymoon suite, I will keep a note of their room number. I wouldn't sleep in a new room, why should they?

DAN: [*Bows.*] Thank you, Your Majesty.

MOLLY: [*Curtsies.*] Thank you, Your Majesty.

QUEEN: And now by virtue of being Queen of all the Helmsleys, I pronounce you husband and wife. Congratulations! You may kiss the bride.

[DAN *kisses* MOLLY. *There are cheers and the band begins to play "Lullaby of Broadway." Five hundred men in top hats and tails begin to tap down the aisle.*]

EPILOGUE

NARRATOR: Dan and Molly became bi-island (Manhattan and Long), with bi-point three children (a girl, a boy, and an au pair from Barnard), and bi-career (a shift into management for him, a cottage industry for her). As Molly approached middle age she began to consult crystals about her hormonal convergence and undertook frequent pilgrimages to Stonehenge. Dan continued to pursue his interest in early American comestibles, and was featured on the cover of *Just Say Cheese* magazine for his distinguished cellar of American pasteurized-cheese foods.

The fortunes of the Queen, however, followed a crueler path. After a long and glorious reign, she was found to be poaching, thereby violating the charter, and was forced to abdicate. Even a monarch must obey the laws of the realm. On the day she was dethroned, she received a monogrammed Cartier sympathy note from Molly.

Dear Your Majesty,

Dan and I send you our best wishes at this difficult time.

Molly

P.S. Is your estate in Greenwich for sale? Also, did you get a kickback from the band at our wedding?

Molly's mother had taught her that a lady always sends a note.

Otherwise — apart from twenty years of couples therapy, his-and-her reconstructive surgery, one triple bypass, and four extramarital affairs — they lived happily ever after.

Lanford Wilson

ABSTINENCE
A Turn

" . . . Abstinence engenders maladies."
Love's Labour's Lost

ABSTINENCE

Lanford Wilson

Lanford Wilson received the 1980 Pulitzer Prizxe for Drama and the New York Drama Critics Circle Award for *Talley's Folly*. He is a founding member of the Circle Repertory Company and one of twenty-one resident playwrights for the company.

His work at Circle Rep includes: *The Family Continues* (1972), *The HOT L Baltimore* (1973), *The Moundbuilders* (1975), *Serenading Louie* (1976), *5th of July* (1978), *Talley's folly* (1980), *A Tale Told* (1981), *Angels Fall* (1982), all directed by Marshall Mason, and the one-act plays *Brontosaurus* (1977) and *Thymus Vulgaris* (1982).

His other plays include: *Balm in Gilead* (1965), *The Gingham Dog* (1966), *The Rimers of Eldritch* (1967), *Lemon Sky* (1969) and some twenty produced one-acts. He has also written the libretto for Lee Hoiby's opera of Tennessee Williams' *Summer and Smoke*, and two television plays, *Taxi!* and *The Migrants* (based on a short story by Tennessee Williams).

Other awards include the New York Critics' Award, the Outer Critcs Circle Award and an Obie for *The HOT L Baltimore*, an Obie for *The Mound Builders*, a Drama-Logue Award for *5th of July* and *Talley's Folly*, the Vernon Rice Award for *The Rimers of Eldritch*, and Tony nominations for *Talley's Folly*, *5th of July*, and *Angels Fall*. He is the recipient of the Brandies University Creative Arts Award in Theatre Arts and the Institute of Arts and Letters Award.

Mr. Wilson has recently completed an entirely new translation of Chekhov's *The Three Sisters*, which was commissioned and produced by the Hartford Stage Company. His play, *Talley and Son* (the third play in the Talley Trilogy) opened in New York on September 24, 1985.

His new plays, *Burn This*, opened at the Mark Taper Forum in Los Angeles in January 1987 starring John Malkovich and Joan Allen and opened on Broadway in October 1987 with the same cast. He is currently writing the screenplay for the film version.

He makes his home in Sag Harbor, New York. *Burn This* was done in London, starring John Malkovich in 1990.

CHARACTERS

    Martha, the Maid, a maid.

    Lon, Winnie's husband. Thirty-five and mild.

    Winnie, thirty, sweet and charming. Always.

    Danna, thirty. Sharp and a little hysterical just tonight.

    Joe, thirty. The All American Sweetheart of a man. Unfortunately crazy.

SCENE: *The very dark front hall of a New York apartment. Maybe track lighting. Chic.*

    [MARTHA, *the Maid, stands at the front door.* LON *enters, lighting a cigarette.*]

LON: I think all the guests are here, Martha.

MARTHA: Is this the shoplifters or the smokers or the sex-offenders or the drunks?

LON: I think it's the weight-watchers, but just in case it's the smokers I stepped out here to have a cigarette.

WINNIE: [*Enters from another way.*] Happy anniversary, darling. I'm so thankful you're here.

LON: Happy anniversary, Winnie. My helpful little helpless wife. I thought you were in with your guests.

WINNIE: I just popped up for a moment to tuck in the children.

LON: Why is it that every anniversary we have to give a party for one of your charity groups?

WINNIE: I just feel our life is so perfect we should help those less fortunate.

    [*They exit arm in arm.*]

MARTHA: [*To the audience.*] Already you know we're in trouble, right?

    [*The doorbell rings.* MARTHA *reaches to open it, turns to look at audience.*]

    One tip. Always bet on somebody named Winnie.

    [*She opens the door.* DANNA *staggers in a step.*]

DANNA: Thank God someone's here! You're not Winnie. You're ... she talks about you all the time ... you're Abigail or Eleanor or Lady Bird. . . .

MARTHA: Martha.

DANNA: Martha!

MARTHA: And whom should I say . . .?

DANNA: Oh. I'm a friend. I've just come from a meeting — this is the closest place I could think of. Tell her — My name is — God, I knew it a minute ago. Danna! I'm Danna Walsh.

MARTHA: Danna Walsh. [*In one move* MARTHA *takes a book from nowhere, pages quickly to the back, checks, raises her eyebrows.*]

DANNA: Now, Jackie, darling . . .

MARTHA: Martha.

DANNA: Martha, darling, you've got to get me a drink.

MARTHA: No way.

DANNA: I'll give you money. I'll give you my jewels. I'll give you my husband — no, I dumped him, I'll give you my mother.

MARTHA: I was weakening but you blew it.

WINNIE: [*Entering.*] Martha, who was at — Danna, darling! I so wanted to be there for you tonight but we have this dinner party every year.

DANNA: I hate to burst in on you like this but you've always been so helpful. I have to talk to you alone.

WINNIE: Oh, Martha knows everything.

DANNA: You do?

[*Beat. Goes to* MARTHA.]

What is a . . .

[*Whispers.* MARTHA *raises her eyebrows, whispers back into* DANNA'S *ear.*]

Well, of course it is. It's absurdly simple if you think about it.

[*To* WINNIE.]

Winnie, you've got to help me.

WINNIE: You don't look well at all. How did it go?

DANNA: How did what go?

WINNIE: The meeting. A.A. The first anniversary of your sobriety.

DANNA: Who remembers, it must have been twenty minutes ago. I was a wreck. I qualified. Everyone applauded. I could have ripped their hearts out. I was congratulated. The rich bitch who runs things called me a brick. I've never wanted a drink so badly in my life.

WINNIE: Don't be silly. We're all so proud of you! You've gone an entire year today without a drink.

DANNA: A year? Are you mad? What would be so unusual about that? This is leap year, you idiot. Three hundred sixty-six long tedious days. And three hundred sixty-six long hopeless nights. I've read over five hundred books. I've written four. I've knitted some things: a bed cover, wallpaper for the living room. Johnnie Walker Red! Now there's a man with spine. Aren't you going to ask me in?

WINNIE: You're in, darling.

DANNA: This is your apartment? This well? It's pitch in here!

WINNIE: Would you like a cup of tea?

DANNA: [*All hope gone. Musing.*] Oh ... no ... I've been haunted all day by a scene in one of the Thin Man movies. Nick is at the table when Nora comes in late, and she asks him how much he's had to drink; Nick says he's had five martinis. And when the waiter comes over Nora says, "Would you please bring me five martinis?"

[*Beat.*]

I want to live like that. I want charm in my life. I want my alcohol back. I used to have a wonderful life. I mean, I didn't have friends, but I didn't notice.

WINNIE: Why don't you come join us? Just twenty or so, they're sitting down to eat. They're Liars, I'm afraid, Liars Anonymous, but you know how charming they can be.

DANNA: Food? How shallow. People don't know? Without a drink? I'll just steady myself against the wall here — where is it? — and I'll be fine. If Dolly could just bring me a ...

MARTHA: Forget it.

WINNIE: I know, love. I'm a drunk, too. I've had some —

DANNA: Ha! You call yourself a drunk? You haven't had a drink in three years. Put me in front of a bottle of Cuervo Gold and I'll show you a drunk.

WINNIE: You know what we say: One day at a time.

DANNA: I've experienced one day at a time for three hundred sixty-six days — end to end. Twenty-four hours in every day, eighty-six thousand four hundred seconds. I know, I counted them once. A year ago I could celebrate the Fourth of July, come home, go to bed, wake up, it would be November.

LON: [*Enters. Sees* DANNA, *maybe hesitates one step, smiles.*] Winnie, are you coming back to the . . .

WINNIE: Lon, I want you to meet a dear friend of mine. This is Danna. We've been friends for, oh, my, how long is it?

DANNA: Three hundred sixty-six . . . endless . . .

WINNIE: Is it a year already? Danna, this is my husband, Lon.

DANNA: You don't happen to be carrying, do you?

WINNIE: Danna was just admiring the foyer.

LON: Yes, my wife did the entire apartment herself.

DANNA: I haven't seen it.

LON: I was just talking to the most remarkable man in there. He says he climbed Mount Everest completely by himself.

WINNIE: Let me just — oh, you know what a terrible organizer I am — I'll just get the next course started and then I'm all yours.

[*She goes out, smiling. Just before she leaves she stops. Thinks. Looks at* MARTHA, *then goes out thinking. A calm beat. You can't tell, but they are listening to* WINNIE'S *retreat*]

DANNA: [*They stare at each other an intense moment. Then:*] Alonzo!

[*They kiss passionately, fall to the ground in a 69 position,* LON'S *head up* DANNA'S *dress, both growling and barking like dogs. They sit up.* DAN-NA'S *hair is a mess. They stare at each other a frozen beat.*]

MARTHA: [*To audience*] I turned down a paying job to do this play.

LON: [*To* DANNA] Every moment without you has been hell!

DANNA: You can't possibly be Winnie's husband. You're that pompous miser she talks about? She said you were eighty! She said you had no teeth.

LON: Where did you meet Winnie?

DANNA: Ha! You think she really goes to ballet class five times a week? Have you once asked to see her plié? You told me your wife was

Catholíc, blind, and confined to a wheelchair.

LON: I didn't want to worry you.

DANNA: I mean she's a kind-hearted helpless thing, but you might have told me you were married to Miss Ripple of 1985.

LON: Don't be jealous, Danna. Winnie never drinks.

DANNA: Ha! I could tell you stories about that Sweet-pea that would turn your piss green. Ever wonder why she carried a sewing basket for twelve years without ever so much as darning a sock?

LON: Winnie is the most charitable woman in the city.

DANNA: If you mean she's known for giving it away.

LON: This is not becoming, Danna.

DANNA: She can't help it, poor dear. While you're down on Wall Street that poor helpless thing is down on half of Spanish Harlem.

LON: You could hardly know her.

DANNA: I know you have two olive-skinned sons with flashing black eyes.

LON: [*Moving closer, becoming aroused.*] If anything, Winnie is almost too gentle and kind. She has none of the shocking terms of endearment that you have. Or the voracious appetite. None of the inventive positions . . . certainly none of the improvisationally creative — before I met you I had no idea of the things that could be done with raw vegetables. If I were to think one of you had a broad experience . . .

DANNA: I wasn't myself, Lon. I was sober. And as for the potato trick, I learned that one at . . . [*Remembering herself.*] I mean to say . . . "Winnie" you said her name was? No, we've only met a couple of times. Meetings or something, a few friends. I had no idea she was your wife. I doubt that I could allow myself to see you again now that I know — [*Losing it.*] — unless you either take me right here in this dungeon of a foyer or bring me a Manhattan. Oh, god! With a Manhattan who needs a man? A Manhattan asks nothing from you. It doesn't deceive or sulk or play games. And it has, God knows, more interesting conversation. A Manhattan . . . listens!

LON: [*Love talk.*] You said to pick —

[LON *shuts up as* WINNIE *enters. She notices but doesn't show it.*]

WINNIE: Now, I'm all yours.

DANNA: Winnie! You poor deceived darling. You weak and caring . . .

WINNIE: Could you wait just a little moment? [*She exits.*]

LON: [*Adjusting back.*] You said to pick up a zuccini . . . I got three. And a cucumber. And a baby eggplant. And a crooked necked squash. The mind boggles.

DANNA: [*Torn, but.*] Woah . . . no, no Lon. It's not enough. The night with the pumpkin was fun, but it's not enough.

LON: Martha might ask the cook if she has any sherry.

MARTHA: This woman is loaded for bear, she'd blow a glass of sherry to hell.

LON: Really, I don't believe there's any alcohol in the house.

DANNA: You're goddamned right there isn't. You'll find there's no nail polish remover either. That tit-mouse wouldn't trust herself in the same room with vanilla extract. Why do you think the radiator kept freezing on your car? It's the trusting ones who need our help, Alonzo. She needs you. A charming intelligent dynamo of a man who inherited thirty-seven million and has parlayed that, now, into . . . how much?

LON: [*Proud.*] Well . . . a little over twelve. But I could never leave you. You're special. Who else has a living room with cable-knit walls?

DANNA: [*Pleased.*] For one, my mother. I did hers too.

LON: But, you're right. Winnie does need me.

DANNA: If it were anyone but that lovely, uncomplicated . . .

LON: But she doesn't have to know.

DANNA: The woman has gimlet eyes. She's been sober for three years, she can see through six feet of concrete.

[WINNIE *enters with* JOE, *a very handsome young man indeed.*]

WINNIE: Danna, darling. I wanted you to meet Joe. Joe is a friend of Bill Wilson's too.

JOE: Sorry, Winnie, I'd love to meet the fellow but I don't know Bill Wilson at all. Sounds like a lovely guy. Do you?

DANNA: Know him? I've practically had his child. If he were here I'd saute the sanctimonious son-of-a-bitch in Marsala. Whoever — [*She*

notices JOE *for the first time and does not take her eyes off him again.*]
Oh. Hi, Joe.

JOE: Hi.

DANNA: You're leaving soon?

JOE: I don't know. My pilot had the jet warmed up to go to Buenos Aires, but I saw you in the hall here and called him to cancel the trip.

DANNA: And then, Buenos Aires is so . . . hot this time of year.

JOE: And I don't like to fly without a drink and my doctor says my liver's shot. All those years in the P.O.W camps.

DANNA: You poor dear. What was your drink? Bourbon?

JOE: Well, since we have our own vineyards, I mostly just stick to Dom Perignon. Family loyalty and all that.

DANNA: With me it's a cold vodka martini. Or two.

JOE: Twist or an olive?

DANNA: Hold the garbage.

JOE: So this is your anniversary.

DANNA: My first. It's been little nervous-making.

WINNIE: Remember, you don't have to worry about tomorrow. You just have to get through tonight.

DANNA: Oh, suddenly, I don't think that's going to be such a problem. — I don't know though. You sound like a playboy.

JOE: Actually, I'm a physicist.

DANNA: My.

[WINNIE *is helping* JOE *on with his coat.*]

JOE: And you live close by.

DANNA: Twenty or thirty blocks.

LON: Danna? Aren't you going to say goodnight? Danna? The crisper?

WINNIE: Oh. And Joe.

JOE: Yes, Winnie?

WINNIE: Happy anniversary.

JOE: Thanks.

DANNA: It's your anniversary too?

JOE: Well, I don't talk about it. My wife, the Duchess, had a passion for collecting Iranian pottery. Nothing would do but she had to go there just one more time.

DANNA: Oh, no.

JOE: Caught in a terrorist crossfire.

DANNA: You don't have to talk about it.

JOE: Should we walk?

DANNA: Let's take a cab.

[*They leave.*]

WINNIE: [*After a beat.*] I do hope she'll be all right.

LON: You worry too much about other people. She can look after herself. Not like my helpless darling. It's his anniversary, too?

WINNIE: Yes. Such a pity. But they let him out this one night every year. We must go in and join our guests . . . take my arm. Now, remember, this is my Liars Anonymous group; don't believe a word anyone says . . . Darling. I was looking in the refrigerator. You must show me what you plan to do with all those vegetables.

[MARTHA *is left alone as at the beginning. A pause.*]

MARTHA: . . . "The night with the pumpkin . . . was fun? . . ." [*Beat.*] Liars Anonymous. Wouldn't you know. I had two marriage proposals and a tip on the market from that group.

[*Starts to go, stops.*]

I don't belong to any of those organizations. I don't have the constitution for self-denial. Pity about Joe not being a physicist. Just as well, though. I don't trust scientists. They say they can put your body in cold storage for a hundred years and thaw you out as a good as now? Come on. I mean have you ever tasted freeze-dried coffee? [*Going.*] What a nasty little play. I don't know about you but I'll never touch a crudité again. [*Gone.*]

DUO!
The Best Scenes for the 90's
Edited by John Horvath & Lavonne Mueller

DUO! delivers a collection of scenes for two so hot they sizzle. Each scene has been selected as a freestanding dramatic unit offering two actors a wide range of theatrical challenge and opportunity.

Every scene is set up with a synopsis of the play, character descriptions, and notes. DUO! offers a full spectrum of age range, region, genre, character, level of difficulty, and non-traditional casting potential. Among the selections:

EMERALD CITY · BURN THIS · BROADWAY BOUND
EASTERN STANDARD · THE HEIDI CHRONICLES
JOE TURNER'S COME AND GONE
RECKLESS · PSYCHO BEACH PARTY
FRANKIE & JOHNNY IN THE CLAIR DE LUNE
COASTAL DISTURBANCES · THE SPEED OF DARKNESS
LES LIAISONS DANGEREUSES · LETTICE AND LOVAGE
THE COCKTAIL HOUR · BEIRUT
M. BUTTERFLY · DRIVING MISS DAISY · MRS KLEIN
A GIRL'S GUIDE TO CHAOS · A WALK IN THE WOODS
THE ROAD TO MECCA · BOY'S LIFE · SAFE SEX
LEND ME A TENOR · A SHAYNA MAIDEL · ICE CREAM
SPEED-THE-PLOW · OTHER PEOPLE'S MONEY
CUBA AND HIS TEDDY BEAR

paper · ISBN: 1-55783-030-4

❦APPLAUSE❦

MONOLOGUE WORKSHOP
From Search to Discovery
in Audition and Performance
by Jack Poggi

To those for whom the monologue has always been synonymous with terror, *The Monologue Workshop* will prove an indispensable ally. Jack Poggi's new book answers the long-felt need among actors for top-notch guidance in finding, rehearsing, and performing monologues. For those who find themselves groping for a speech just hours before their "big break," this book is their guide to salvation.

The Monologue Workshop supplies the tools to discover new pieces before they become over-familiar, excavate older material that has been neglected, and adapt material from non-dramatic sources (novels, short stories, letters, diaries, autobiographies, even newspaper columns). There are also chapters on writing original monologues and creating solo performances in the style of Lily Tomlin and Eric Bogosian.

Besides the wealth of practical advice he offers, Poggi transforms the monologue experience from a terrifying ordeal into an exhilarating opportunity. Jack Poggi, as many working actors will attest, is the actor's partner in a process they had always thought was without one.

paper • ISBN: 1-55783-031-2

❦APPLAUSE❧

OTHER PEOPLE'S MONEY
By Jerry Sterner

Best Off-Broadway Play of 1989: Outer Critics Circle

"*Other People's Money* is an extraordinarily insightful, timely and witty play."

— Donald Trump

"The best new play I've run across all season. It would stand out in any year."

— Douglas Watt
DAILY NEWS

"*Other People's Money* has a heart of iron which beats about the cannibalistic nature of big business."

— Mel Gussow
THE NEW YORK TIMES

"Some of the funniest lines I've heard in a long time . . . many, I find myself repeating."

— Carl Icahn

"Mesmerizing! A fascinating, completely convincing portrayal of a man for whom money is the ultimate seduction!"

— UPI

paper • ISBN: 1-55783-061-4   cloth • ISBN: 1-55783-062-2

❦APPLAUSE❦

SQUARE ONE
A Play by Steve Tesich

The Oscar-winning author of *Breaking Away*

With *Square One*, Steve Tesich once again moves us further onto a frightening frontier of the twentieth century. He discovers the brutal social rhythms of conformity as they rise up to silence the unique impulses and creative reflexes of modern man. While most contemporary dramatists are content to putter around their neighbors' gardens in order to sniff out the garden variety of domestic calamity, Tesich creates a highly sophisticated hybrid of contemporary existence to give us a terrifying whiff of the future.

"An achingly sad, brutal, futuristic comedy that is strangely sweet as often as it is chilling."
　　　　　　　　　—Linda Winer, NEWSDAY

"The most memorable play to hit off-Broadway this season."　　　—John Harris, THEATERWEEK

"A brave new world where nothing is particularly brave or particularly new. . . . IT IS A WARNING. Do see it. I suspect you owe it to yourself and somehow to our communal future."
　　　　　　　　　—Clive Barnes, NEW YORK POST

Steve Tesich is the author of many plays including *Division Street* and *The Speed of Darkness*. He won the Academy Award for Best Screenplay for *Breaking Away*. He divides his time between Manhattan and Colorado.

paper • ISBN: 1-55783-076-2

❀APPLAUSE❀

I AM A WOMAN
Conceived and Arranged by
Viveca Lindfors & Paul Austin

"Lindfors delivered a revelation . . . her essential subject was not morality but love. It is precisely this sort of theatre that they ought to bring all people to these days."
— NEWSWEEK

I Am a Woman, performed by Viveca Lindfors in a widely acclaimed one-woman show, charts the journey of one woman through the voices of many renowned authors. Thirty-six unique women collectively express a journey of awakening feminine consciousness. For reading or performing, here is a repertoire of the heart. Among the excerpts:

PENTIMENTO Hellman • DIARY OF ANNE FRANK Frank • LADY CHATTERLY'S LOVER Lawrence • A CONVERSATION AGAINST DEATH Merriam • THE LIBERATED ORGASM Seaman • LITTLE GIRL MY STRINGBEAN MY LOVELY WOMAN Sexton • DANCE OF DEATH Strindberg • IN MY MOTHER'S HOUSE Colette • THE MADWOMAN OF CHAILLOT Giraudoux • LOVERS AND OTHER STRANGERS Taylor & Bologna • MISALLIANCE Shaw

paper • ISBN: 1-55783-048-7

❦APPLAUSE❦

ANTIGONE
by Bertolt Brecht
A Play
With selections from Brecht's Model Book
Translated by Judith Malina

Sophocles, Hölderlin, Brecht, Malina — four major figures in the world's theatre — they have all left their imprint on this remarkable dramatic text. Friedrich Hölderlin translated Sophocles into German, Brecht adapted Hölderlin, and now Judith Malina has rendered Brecht's version into a stunning English incarnation.

Brecht's *Antigone* is destined to be performed, read and discussed across the English-speaking world.

AVAILABLE FOR THE FIRST TIME IN ENGLISH

paper • ISBN: 0-936839-25-2

✿APPLAUSE✿